# FERMENTING
# FOOD STEP BY STEP

# FERMENTING
# FOOD STEP BY STEP

Adam Elabd

DK | Penguin Random House

*To my grandmother, who taught me the love, common sense, and joy of cooking. She also makes a mean pickle.*

**British Edition**
**Project Editor:** Kathryn Meeker
**Senior Art Editor:** Glenda Fisher
**Angliciser:** Susannah Steel
**Jacket Designer:** Harriet Yeomans
**Managing Editor:** Stephanie Farrow
**Managing Art Editor:** Christine Keilty
**Pre-production Producers:** Rebecca Fallowfield & Tony Phipps
**Senior Producer:** Stephanie McConnell
**Creative Technical Support:** Sonia Charbonnier

**American Edition**
**Publisher:** Mike Sanders
**Associate Publisher:** Billy Fields
**Senior Acquisitions Editor:** Brook Farling
**Development Editor:** Ann Barton
**Designer:** XAB Design
**Photographer:** Ali Donzé Photography
**Food Stylist:** Joe Lazo
**Proofreader:** Michelle Melani
**Indexer:** Brad Herriman

First published in Great Britain in 2016 by
Dorling Kindersley Limited
80 Strand, London, WC2R 0RL

A CIP catalogue record for this book is available from the British Library.
ISBN: 978-0-2412-4066-3

Printed and bound in China.

All images © Dorling Kindersley Limited
For further information see: www.dkimages.com

A WORLD OF IDEAS:
SEE ALL THERE IS TO KNOW
www.dk.com

# CONTENTS

**Chapter 1: Getting started** . . . . . . . . . . . . 8
What is fermentation? . . . . . . . . . . . . . . . . . 10
A global tradition . . . . . . . . . . . . . . . . . . . . 12
Why ferment? . . . . . . . . . . . . . . . . . . . . . . 14
Types of ferments . . . . . . . . . . . . . . . . . . . . 16
Essential equipment . . . . . . . . . . . . . . . . . . 18
Fermentation vessels . . . . . . . . . . . . . . . . . . 20
Sourcing ingredients . . . . . . . . . . . . . . . . . . 22
Ideal fermentation environments . . . . . . . . 24
Checking your ferments . . . . . . . . . . . . . . . . 26

**Chapter 2: Vegetables and fruits** . . . . . 28
Pickling . . . . . . . . . . . . . . . . . . . . . . . . . . . 30
Continuous pickle . . . . . . . . . . . . . . . . . . . . 32
Turmeric & carrot pickle . . . . . . . . . . . . . . . 33
Egyptian preserved lemon . . . . . . . . . . . . . . 34
Lift (Egyptian pickled turnips) . . . . . . . . . . . 36
Basic knife techniques . . . . . . . . . . . . . . . . 38
Sunomono (Japanese pickled cucumber) . . . 40
Umeboshi (pickled ume plum) . . . . . . . . . . . 42
Pickled garlic . . . . . . . . . . . . . . . . . . . . . . . 44
Pickled ginger . . . . . . . . . . . . . . . . . . . . . . 45
Sauerkraut . . . . . . . . . . . . . . . . . . . . . . . . . 46
Seaweed kraut . . . . . . . . . . . . . . . . . . . . . . 50
Masala kraut . . . . . . . . . . . . . . . . . . . . . . . 51
Root kraut . . . . . . . . . . . . . . . . . . . . . . . . . 52
Curtido . . . . . . . . . . . . . . . . . . . . . . . . . . . 54
Kimchi . . . . . . . . . . . . . . . . . . . . . . . . . . . . 56
Pak choi white kimchi . . . . . . . . . . . . . . . . . 60
Slicing, peeling, & grating techniques . . . . . 62
Pickled tomatoes . . . . . . . . . . . . . . . . . . . . 64
Pickled aubergine . . . . . . . . . . . . . . . . . . . . 65
Lahpet (Burmese pickled tea leaves) . . . . . . 66

**Chapter 3: Condiments** . . . . . . . . . . . . 68
Ketchup . . . . . . . . . . . . . . . . . . . . . . . . . . . 70
Mole ketchup . . . . . . . . . . . . . . . . . . . . . . . 72
Horseradish . . . . . . . . . . . . . . . . . . . . . . . . 73
Mustard . . . . . . . . . . . . . . . . . . . . . . . . . . . 74
More ways to use condiments . . . . . . . . . . . 76
Sauerkraut mustard . . . . . . . . . . . . . . . . . . 78

Dijon mustard . . . . . . . . . . . . . . . . . . . . . . . 79
Jalapeño hot sauce . . . . . . . . . . . . . . . . . . 80
Wild habanero hot sauce . . . . . . . . . . . . . 82
Cashew spread . . . . . . . . . . . . . . . . . . . . . . 84
Sweet onion relish . . . . . . . . . . . . . . . . . . 86
Tamarind date chutney . . . . . . . . . . . . . . . 87
Cultured coconut cream . . . . . . . . . . . . . 88
Coconut chutney . . . . . . . . . . . . . . . . . . . . 90

**Chapter 4: Dairy** . . . . . . . . . . . . . . . . . **.92**
Cultured butter . . . . . . . . . . . . . . . . . . . . . . 94
Cultured buttermilk . . . . . . . . . . . . . . . . . . 96
Kefir . . . . . . . . . . . . . . . . . . . . . . . . . . . . . . . 98
Yogurt . . . . . . . . . . . . . . . . . . . . . . . . . . . . 100
Greek yogurt . . . . . . . . . . . . . . . . . . . . . . 104
Sour cream . . . . . . . . . . . . . . . . . . . . . . . . 105
Simple cheesemaking equipment . . . . . . . 106
Labneh . . . . . . . . . . . . . . . . . . . . . . . . . . . 108
Chevre . . . . . . . . . . . . . . . . . . . . . . . . . . . 110
Queso fresco . . . . . . . . . . . . . . . . . . . . . . 112

**Chapter 5: Legumes and grains** . . . . . **114**
Natto (Japanese fermented soybean) . . . . 116
Amazake (fermented rice ) . . . . . . . . . . . . 118
Dosa . . . . . . . . . . . . . . . . . . . . . . . . . . . . . 120
Uttapam . . . . . . . . . . . . . . . . . . . . . . . . . . 124
Soaking & sprouting seeds, beans,
    & grains . . . . . . . . . . . . . . . . . . . . . . . 126
Sprouted grains . . . . . . . . . . . . . . . . . . . . 128
Rejuvelac . . . . . . . . . . . . . . . . . . . . . . . . . 129
Tofu . . . . . . . . . . . . . . . . . . . . . . . . . . . . . . 130
Tha Bai (Cambodian fermented rice) . . . . 132
Nixtamal . . . . . . . . . . . . . . . . . . . . . . . . . . 134

**Chapter 6: Bread** . . . . . . . . . . . . . . . . **136**
Gorditas . . . . . . . . . . . . . . . . . . . . . . . . . . 138
Injera . . . . . . . . . . . . . . . . . . . . . . . . . . . . . 140
Buckwheat buttermilk pancakes . . . . . . . . 142
Making & using sourdough starters . . . . . . 144
Sourdough bread . . . . . . . . . . . . . . . . . . . 146
Sourdough pizza . . . . . . . . . . . . . . . . . . . 150
Purple amazake sourdough . . . . . . . . . . . 152

**Chapter 7: Beverages** . . . . . . . . . . . . . **154**
Ginger bug . . . . . . . . . . . . . . . . . . . . . . . . 156
Herbal syrup . . . . . . . . . . . . . . . . . . . . . . 157
Bottling & carbonating . . . . . . . . . . . . . . . 158
Ginger beer . . . . . . . . . . . . . . . . . . . . . . . 160
Tepache . . . . . . . . . . . . . . . . . . . . . . . . . . 162
Amazake horchata . . . . . . . . . . . . . . . . . . 164
Water kefir . . . . . . . . . . . . . . . . . . . . . . . . 166
Coconut water kefir . . . . . . . . . . . . . . . . . 167
Pineapple ginger kefir . . . . . . . . . . . . . . . 168
Starting & sharing SCOBYs . . . . . . . . . . . 170
Kombucha . . . . . . . . . . . . . . . . . . . . . . . . 172
Earl Grey cherry kombucha . . . . . . . . . . . 176
Colonche (fermented prickly pear) . . . . . 178
Jun (fermented tea with honey) . . . . . . . . 179
Beetroot kvass . . . . . . . . . . . . . . . . . . . . . 180
Coconut milk kefir . . . . . . . . . . . . . . . . . . 182

**Chapter 8: Alcohol** . . . . . . . . . . . . . . . **184**
Hard ginger beer . . . . . . . . . . . . . . . . . . . 186
Kefir champagne . . . . . . . . . . . . . . . . . . . 188
Hard cider . . . . . . . . . . . . . . . . . . . . . . . . . 190
Spiced hard cider . . . . . . . . . . . . . . . . . . . 194
Mead . . . . . . . . . . . . . . . . . . . . . . . . . . . . . 196
Raspberry mead . . . . . . . . . . . . . . . . . . . . 197
Customizing your brews . . . . . . . . . . . . . . 198
Mandarin wine . . . . . . . . . . . . . . . . . . . . . 200
Sato . . . . . . . . . . . . . . . . . . . . . . . . . . . . . . 202
Date wine . . . . . . . . . . . . . . . . . . . . . . . . . 204

**Chapter 9: Vinegar** . . . . . . . . . . . . . . . **206**
Pineapple cider vinegar . . . . . . . . . . . . . . 208
Red wine vinegar . . . . . . . . . . . . . . . . . . . 210
Making herbal vinegars . . . . . . . . . . . . . . 212
Infused vinegar . . . . . . . . . . . . . . . . . . . . 214
Fire cider . . . . . . . . . . . . . . . . . . . . . . . . . . 216

Index . . . . . . . . . . . . . . . . . . . . . . . . . . . . . 218

# INTRODUCTION

Fermenting food is an exciting journey, full of unexpected side roads, interesting discoveries, and uniquely satisfying results. My main goal and wish is that you have fun with fermentation. If you open up to it and allow it to do so, fermentation will become a regular part of food preparation and interaction in your home. At its core, fermentation is simple, safe, and practical.

Take this book not as a list of recipes for specific fermentations, but as a manual for understanding the basic principles behind several different types of fermentation. I have tried to include a range of methods and techniques that you can study and apply to whatever suits your fancy. I never do anything the same way twice and prefer to open my fermentation and creation to the infinite possibility of the moment. Instead of trying to pin down the "perfect" sauerkraut, allow each batch to be a perfect expression of your kitchen, pantry, thoughts, feelings, and abundance in different moments in time.

For me, the main benefit of making your own food is the depth of connection that you gain from spending time with it. Allow that time to be free flowing and true to who you are and what you have been provided.

## USiNG THiS BOOK

This book isn't necessarily intended to be read in order from front to back; it's meant to be explored. Most of the ferments can be made with nothing more than a few simple ingredients and a little bit of patience, but there are a few recipes that require another recipe as an ingredient. In these cases, the recipe names appear in boldface type on the ingredients list, so you'll know to look for them elsewhere in the book.

# GETTING STARTED

A little foundational knowledge is important to have if you want to be successful with your ferments. In this chapter, you'll learn the basic facts about fermentation, a little history behind the process, what tools and equipment you'll need, how to source your ingredients, and more.

# WHAT IS FERMENTATION?

Fermentation is akin to alchemy. Given the right conditions, simple ingredients can come together and undergo a transformation to become something entirely different and new.

## WINE

Grapes are transformed into wine when they are crushed and the naturally occurring yeast on the grape skins feasts on the sugars.

**YEAST**        **GRAPES**

## BEER

When yeast is added to malted grains, such as barley or wheat, the yeast consumes the sugars to create beer.

**YEAST**        **MALTED GRAIN**

## FROM FRESH TO FERMENTED

When microorganisms, known as the "starter", are introduced to the carbohydrates in food and kept under certain conditions for an extended period of time, fermentation takes place. These microorganisms, such as yeast or bacteria, convert carbohydrates in foods, such as starches or sugars, into alcohols or acids. The alcohols or acids serve as a natural preservative. This process transforms the characteristics of foods, often deepening colours, softening textures, introducing pungent aromas, and producing tangy or sour flavours. The end product of the fermentation process depends on both the type of starter introduced as well as the food to which the fermentation occurs, but the result is a new type of food that is naturally preserved, with deeper, more intense flavours.

## THE IMPORTANCE OF A STARTER

A "starter" is the culture (bacteria, yeast, or mould) that causes fermentation. In some foods, such as vegetables, the starter necessary for fermentation is already present, and all that's required is placing the food in the right environment for fermentation to take place. For other ferments, such as kombucha, the starter must be intentionally introduced.

## SAUERKRAUT

When cabbage and salt are combined and massaged to create a brine, the naturally occurring bacteria present on the cabbage creates sauerkraut.

**BACTERIA**                              **CABBAGE**

## CHEESE

Cheeses of all types involve the introduction of some form of bacteria or mould to transform the milk into something altogether different.

**BACTERIA**                              **MILK**

# A **GLOBAL** TRADITION

The origins of fermentation are as varied as the foods themselves and the diverse cultures they represent. Nearly every culture on the planet uses fermentation in some form.

Fermented foods can be found the world over, and they play an important cultural and practical role in many cuisines. Many ferments are found in similar forms all over the world, while others are unique to specific locations.

## AROUND THE WORLD

Fermenting has roots in cultures from nearly every continent.

**Germany, Poland** Sauerkraut

**Greece** Yogurt

**France** Wine, cheese

**Italy** Balsamic vinegar, prosciutto, salami

**Belgium** Beer

**Mexico** Tepache

**Latin America** Queso fresco

**El Salvador** Curtido

**Peru** Chicha

**Egypt** Pickled lemon

**Ethiopia** Injera, t'ej

**Russia** Kvass

**Burma** Lahpet

**India** Dosa, chutney

**Korea** Kimchi

**China, Far East** Tofu

**Indonesia** Tempeh

**Japan** Miso, amazake, natto

**Mexico** Jalapeños and other chillies have been used to make hot sauce for centuries.

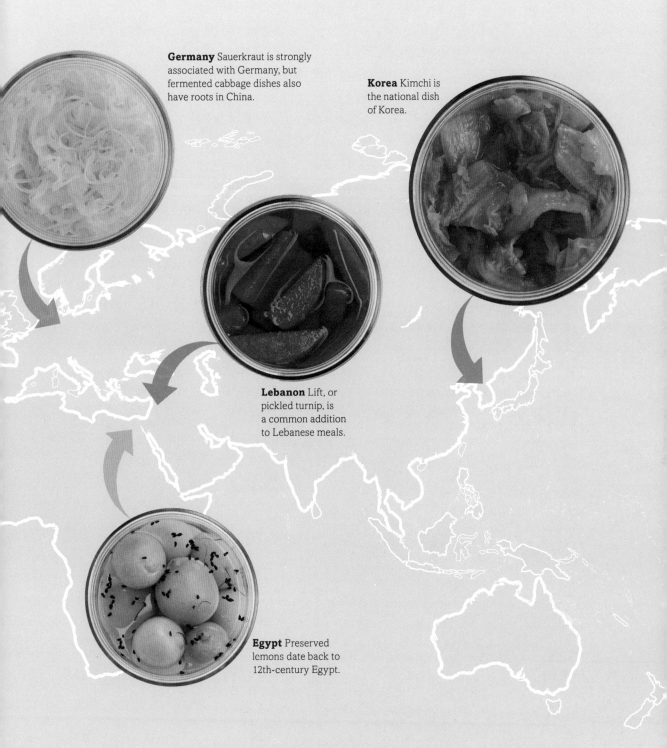

**Germany** Sauerkraut is strongly associated with Germany, but fermented cabbage dishes also have roots in China.

**Korea** Kimchi is the national dish of Korea.

**Lebanon** Lift, or pickled turnip, is a common addition to Lebanese meals.

**Egypt** Preserved lemons date back to 12th-century Egypt.

# WHY FERMENT?

Fermenting at home has many benefits. It's a uniquely satisfying way to preserve food, experiment with bold and exciting flavours, and maintain good digestive health.

## TO PRESERVE

Before refrigeration and pasteurization, fermenting was the primary way for people to preserve perishable foods and access their nutrients year round. Fermentation remains a simple, natural way to extend the life of produce and dairy products without the need for any added preservatives or stabilizers.

## FOR FLAVOUR

Fermentation unlocks a range of complex flavours. Food that may seem bland or unpalatable can become tangy, salty, sour, or sweet. Many of the world's most highly prized foods, including wine, cheese, spirits, and vinegar, are made through fermentation.

## FOR HEALTH

The human gut is home to a wide variety of probiotics – the "good" bacteria that help to maintain balance in our digestive and immune systems and protect us from illness by preventing the growth and spread of harmful bacteria. This gut flora is with us from birth and grows as we age, but healthy gut flora can be diminished by environmental factors, such as the use of

The tradition of fermenting dates back to the **Neolithic period** when fermented fruit was consumed. **Bread, wine, and cheese** are also among the earliest forms of fermented foods.

antibiotics or the consumption of processed foods. Many modern food production practices create sterile conditions, which may help promote public health by killing bad bacteria, but also eliminates the naturally occurring beneficial bacteria we need to maintain healthy, balanced gut flora. Eating fermented foods, which are rich in beneficial bacteria, can help to restore balance and vitality to the microflora in our guts, improving digestive function and strengthening the immune system.

**Protects the body from bacterial infections and illness**

# HEALTHY GUT FLORA

## GUT FLORA IS WITH US FROM BIRTH AND GROWS AS WE AGE

**Supports and strengthens the immune system**

**Allows nutrients in food to be absorbed easily due to the presence of digestive enzymes**

**Reduces digestive issues, such as diarrhoea and constipation**

**Powerful probiotics**
Fermentation requires live, active cultures to convert sugar to alcohol or acid, preserving the food and altering its flavour and texture. These cultures are also beneficial to gut health.

**Preserve almost any food**
Almost any type of food – meats, dairy products, fruits and vegetables, grains – can be preserved through fermentation.

# TYPES OF FERMENTS

Fermentation types are difficult to categorize, because many traditional ferments are not controlled and may have multiple fermentation processes working in unison. However, these are the most common categories of ferments.

## BACTERIAL FERMENTS

**Kimchi**
Kimchi utilizes the naturally occurring bacteria present on vegetables, such as cabbage or turnips. Traditionally, kimchi is packed into earthenware jars and buried underground to ferment for several months.

**Sauerkraut**
The cabbage in sauerkraut contains *Lactobacillus*, a naturally occurring bacteria that is present on most fruits and vegetables.

Bacterial ferments are the most common type and are driven by various strains of **beneficial bacteria**. In most bacterial ferments, the bacteria required to ferment the food is **naturally occurring** and already present on the food itself.

**Yogurt**
Yogurt utilizes two primary strains of bacteria – *Lactobacillus bulgaricus* and *Streptococcus thermophiles*. These beneficial bacteria consume the milk sugar, or lactose, that is present in milk to produce lactic acid.

**Natto**
Natto ferments via a specific hay or grass bacterium (*Bacillus subtilis*) that lives on rice straw.

## MOULD FERMENTS

**Tempeh**
The *Rhizopus oligosporus* mould is a key component in making tempeh, which is a fermented bean cake that is treasured for its high nutritional value.

**Blue cheese**
Blue cheese is made using the *Penicillium* mould strain, which imparts flavour and also gives blue cheese its beautiful blue colour.

Perhaps the **rarest type** of ferment, mould plays a fascinating role in the fermentation process. Many different moulds are used in fermentation, and **each imparts a unique flavour**.

**Sake**
*Aspergillus oryzae,* or koji mould, is used to convert the starches in rice into sugars, which can then be fermented with yeast to make sake.

**Brie**
*Penicillium camemberti* is the mould strain that gives Brie its distinctive flavour. It also produces the flavourful rind that encases the cheese.

# BACTERIAL/YEAST FERMENTS

### Kefir

Kefir is made from kefir "grains", which are small, gelatinous grains of bacteria and yeast that look somewhat like rice, but can contain up to 35 different strains of beneficial bacteria. Kefir grains can be used again and again for making new batches of kefir.

### Kombucha

Kombucha is a tea beverage that utilizes a SCOBY (Symbiotic Colony of Bacteria and Yeast), sugar, and tea. The SCOBY ferments the tea by consuming the sugar, producing a tart and refreshing probiotic beverage.

Some fermentation cultures involve bacteria and yeast **working together in symbiosis**. The starter cultures for these **unique ferments** can vary from SCOBYs to kefir grains to a sourdough starter. Most starters can be **maintained and shared**.

### Sourdough bread

Sourdough begins from a starter created by combining *Lactobacillus* bacteria present in flour and the naturally occurring yeasts in the air. If properly maintained, a sourdough starter can be used and shared for years.

### Tha bai

Commonly known as Cambodian fermented black rice, Tha bai is a unique ferment that actually utilizes three different processes – mould, yeast, and bacteria – to produce a uniquely sweet and slightly alcoholic fermentation.

# YEAST FERMENTS

### Wine

Yeast consumes the naturally occurring sugars in grapes and other fruits to create wine. If air is allowed to get to wine, acetic acid may be produced, which is what turns wine into vinegar.

### Beer

Beer is the result of yeast consuming the sugars in malted grains, such as barley or wheat.

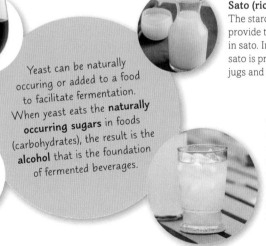

Yeast can be naturally occuring or added to a food to facilitate fermentation. When yeast eats the **naturally occurring sugars** in foods (carbohydrates), the result is the **alcohol** that is the foundation of fermented beverages.

### Sato (rice wine)

The starchy sugars in rice provide the food for the yeast in sato. In some Asian countries sato is produced in earthenware jugs and called *lao hai*.

### Ginger beer

Ginger beer is made using a fermented starter made from fresh ginger and the wild yeast that is present on the ginger root and in the air.

# ESSENTIAL EQUIPMENT

Preparing food for fermentation doesn't require much in the way of special tools. The most important items to have are a sharp, well-made chef's knife and a large cutting board, but there are some specialty tools that can make the job easier.

## COMMON TOOLS

Most of the tools you'll need are probably already in your kitchen. If you have to buy any tools, purchase the highest quality possible.

**Chef's knife** A high-quality chef's knife is a must for preparing vegetables and other ingredients for fermentation.

**Paring knife** A paring knife is handy for peeling vegetables, or making small slices or cuts in ingredients.

**Vegetable peeler** A high-quality vegetable peeler makes the job of peeling much easier.

**Vegetable scrubber or brush** A vegetable scrubber helps remove dirt from cracks and crevices. Look for a brush with thick, dense bristles.

**Grater** Grating carrots and other root vegetables can introduce a different texture to your ferments.

**Microplane** This rasp-style grater can quickly and easily grate tough, fibrous ingredients, like fresh ginger.

**Cutting board** Buy sturdy cutting boards that are large enough to hold large piles. Wood and bamboo are ideal, while glass should be avoided.

**Baking surface** A pizza stone or cast iron baking surface will help to make crusty breads.

## SPECIALTY TOOLS

While most recipes in this book require only common tools, others require some specialty tools. Most of these items can be found at housewares stores or homebrewing supply stores.

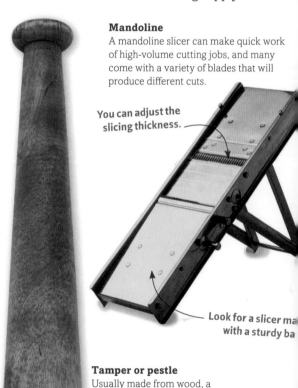

**Mandoline**
A mandoline slicer can make quick work of high-volume cutting jobs, and many come with a variety of blades that will produce different cuts.

You can adjust the slicing thickness.

Look for a slicer ma with a sturdy ba

**Tamper or pestle**
Usually made from wood, a tamper or pestle helps compact ingredients into jars.

A water barrier keeps air out of the vessel.

There are many types of ferments, such as cheeses, that require **further specialty equipment**. This is covered in more detail in each section.

**Airlock**
Airlocks keep air out of carboys while allowing the gasses to escape. Find them at brewing supply stores.

Look for a medium to large volume scale.

**Blender**
Look for a powerful blender with a wide mouth for easier cleaning.

**Funnel**
A small funnel is needed to fit into narrow-necked vessles like swing stopper bottles.

**Scale**
A kitchen scale allows you to measure incredients precisely when baking sourdough breads.

# FERMENTATION
# VESSELS

Choosing a vessel is the first step in creating the proper environment for your ferment. There are a variety of vessels to choose from, each suited to different types of ferments.

When shopping for fermenting vessels, glass is generally the best choice. Glass resists the stains and odours that are produced by the fermentation process, and it doesn't corrode.

Buy high-quality swing stopper bottles with thick rubber band seals that make them airtight.

When fermenting for longer than one week, **use non-corrosive lids for kilner jars.** Steel lids can begin to rust when exposed for an extended period of time to the salt and acids of fermentation.

A 2-litre (2-quart) kilner jar can be used for many types of ferments.

## KILNER JARS

Clear glass kilner jars are an ideal vessel for many types of ferments. It's easy to see the contents and track the progress of fermentation, they come in a variety of standard sizes, and they are impervious to odours and stains. The only downside is fragility; the glass can break easily.

**Best for:** lacto-fermented vegetables, fermented dairy, alcoholic beverages, vinegars

## SWING STOPPER BOTTLES

Alcoholic beverages often undergo further fermentation and carbonation after bottling. Swing stopper bottles provide a tight seal and can be reused multiple times.

**Best for:** fermented beverages

A basic sterilized siphon tube is needed to drain the liquid from the demijohn.

## STERILIZING

Any equipment used for fermenting must be thoroughly sterilized before use to prevent contamination. Prepare all vessels and equipment using the hot wash cycle of a dishwasher or use mild, unscented washing up liquid (one that is not antibacterial) and very hot water. Rinse well to remove any soapy residue.

The channel is filled with water to create a seal that keeps air out, but allows gasses to escape.

These weights are designed for a tight fit that keeps the food submerged beneath the liquid line.

## GLASS DEMIJOHNS

A demijohn has a narrow neck opening that can easily be plugged with an airlock, making it ideal for alcohol fermentation. Demijohns are available in a range of sizes and can be both glass and plastic, but glass is best for fermenting. Use a bottle brush to clean them thoroughly.

**Best for:** fermented beverages

## CERAMIC WATER CROCKS

The water crock is a traditional style of fermentation vessel that dates back to ancient times. They often utilize a weighting stone to press down ferments. These beautiful vessels can be used for many types of ferments

**Best for:** lacto-fermented vegetables

# SOURCING INGREDIENTS

Good ferments start with high-quality ingredients. When selecting ingredients for the recipes in this book, follow these guidelines in order to achieve the best results and greatest health benefits.

## ORGANIC AND LOCAL

As a general rule, you should always buy ingredients that are grown with a minimum of added chemicals, so organic is often the best choice. Most supermarkets offer large selections of organic products as an alternative to products grown using synthetic pesticides. Look for ingredients that are labelled as certified organic, which means the producer has followed the correct organic growing practices.

Buying local is also a wise choice. Farmer's markets and farm stands often sell organic produce, and buying from source allows you to ask the supplier how your produce was grown. Before purchasing, ask about growing practices and if any chemicals were used.

**Fresh produce** Where possible, purchase organic fruits and vegetables. Synthetic pesticides, herbicides, and fertilizers can have a suppressive effect on the beneficial microorganisms of fermentation. Look for produce that is locally grown, as well. When you eat clean produce from your local farmer's market, you inoculate yourself with local microorganisms.

**Dry ingredients** When purchasing grains, seeds, nuts, and legumes, purchase organic whenever possible. As is the case with other ingredients, anything containing synthetic pesticides, herbicides, and fertilizers can have a suppressive effect on the fermentation process. It may be difficult to find organic dry goods, so look online if you can't find these ingredients locally.

Always use **fresh ingredients** that haven't been canned or frozen. **Canned** produce may contain **contaminants** that can affect the ferment, while frozen may not ferment nearly as well as fresh.

**FRESH PRODUCE**

**DRY INGREDIENTS**

# STARTERS

Many of the recipes in this book call for "starters", the ingredient that introduces the microorganisms needed for fermentation to the food product. Some starters, such as whey, are the product of another ferment. Other starters, such as mesophilic starters (for cheese) or water kefir grains, are commercially available. In most cases, starters can be found in speciality stores or online. Speciality ingredients such as Shanghai yeast balls or koji can be found at ethnic markets or through online sources.

**Dairy** For the purposes of fermentation, all dairy should be sourced from cows that have not been treated with any hormones, antibiotics, or other synthetic drugs. Use whole milk products from pasture-raised animals as often as possible. Pasture-raised cows and goats have been shown to produce healthier milk with more good fats and fewer bad ones.

**Salt** Don't reach for iodized table salt; this refined salt has been stripped of its minerals and contains added iodine, which may inhibit fermentation. Instead, look for naturally derived salt varieties that are rich in minerals. Sea salts come in a range of colours and have unique flavour profiles thanks to beneficial trace minerals. Pickling salt can be used, but may contain anti-caking agents.

**Water** Depending on your area and where you get your water from, your tap water may be treated with high levels of chlorine, fluorine, and other chemicals. Chlorine, in particular, inhibits microorganism growth and imparts an unfavourable flavour. Instead of tap water, use clean, filtered water or spring water for ferments. However, avoid distilled water, which has been stripped of naturally occurring minerals.

DAIRY

SALT

WATER

# IDEAL FERMENTATION ENVIRONMENTS

## WATCH THE LIGHT

Light can interfere with the fermentation process, so it's best to keep ferments in a dark place, especially those that are particularly light sensitive, such as vinegars and kombucha. To minimize the risk of light interference, use an opaque fermentation vessel (such as clay), store in a dark cabinet or closet, or surround the fermentation vessel with a dark fabric.

## FIND THE RIGHT TEMPERATURE

Most ferments have an optimal temperature range. Fermenting below the ideal range can result in the microorganisms becoming dormant, while fermenting above the active range can kill the beneficial microorganisms. Ambient room temperature (18°C–24°C; 65°F–75°F) is within the optimal fermentation range for many ferments, but some require temperature control.

### Staying warm

To keep your ferments warm, create an incubation chamber. A cooler filled with hot water bottles, a pre-warmed oven, or a front-loading food dehydrator all work well for this purpose.

### Keeping cool

Cooling is more difficult and requires a dedicated refrigerator with an independent thermostat control. Plan to start ferments that prefer cooler temperatures when the ambient temperature in your home is most suited for them.

## BE PATIENT

An integral part of fermentation is allowing enough time to pass for the microorganisms to do their work. Krauts, kimchis, and wines that are uninspiring or downright off-putting at first can blossom and mature into delightful creations after several months or years of being left to their own devices.

For long-term ageing, store your ferments in a **dark, cool, and dry place**. **Cellars** and **basements** are ideal, as their temperatures do not fluctuate much with the seasons.

| FERMENT TYPE | FERMENTATION TEMPERATURE | TIME TO FERMENT |
| --- | --- | --- |
| Sauerkraut and kimchi | 10°C–30°C (50°F–80°F) | 4 days to 4 months |
| Pickles | 10°C–30°C (50°F–80°F) | 1 day to 3 months |
| Alcoholic beverages | 16°C–24°C (60°F–75°F) | 1 to 6 months |
| Kombucha and vinegar | 20°C–30°C (70°F–85°F) | 5 to 15 days |
| Yogurt | 38°C–43°C (100°F–110°F) | 12 to 24 hours |
| Natto | 60°C (140°F) | 24 hours |

# CHECKING YOUR FERMENTS

Fermentation can seem like a mysterious process, and it's common to worry about spoilage or contamination. However, if you rely on your senses, you'll soon learn to discern the good from the bad.

## 1 LOOK

Most ferments go through considerable transformation and can look dramatically different before and after fermenting. As the acids of fermentation build up, expect greens to dull, reds and purples to brighten, and yellows and oranges to deepen.

Don't be alarmed by discoloured vegetables, white mould, or yeasty films that may form on the surface of vegetable ferments. In most cases, you can scrape off the discoloured layer and enjoy everything underneath.

**Discard your ferment if you see:**
• Brightly coloured molds
• Black moulds

## 2 SMELL

Fermentation stinks! This is part of the process. Aside from the smell of the ferment itself, you may also catch the scent of different compounds in the gasses released by the ferment. Apples, cabbage and other foods high in sulphur can give off a sulphorous, "rotten-egg" smell mid-way through fermentation, but this will not be present in the final product. However, there are some smells that indicate spoilage.

**Discard your ferment if you smell:**
• Ammonia (except natto)
• Acetone or nail polish
• Rotting or putrid smell

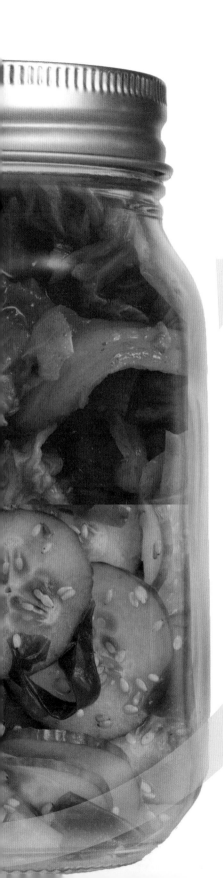

While many people often believe fermented food is spoiled food, it's quite the opposite. Fermented food **truly is preserved**, and it's done so **without any artificial chemicals or additives**.

# 4 TASTE

Fermented foods are often considered delicacies due to the pungent and deep flavours they exhibit. While these may not always be appealing at first, your appetite for the rich flavours, textures, and aromas of fermented foods will develop and grow as you explore different ferments. However, if something really does taste spoiled or rotten, it should not be eaten.

**Discard your ferment if you taste:**
• Rotten or putrid flavours

# 3 TOUCH

While there are several ferments that are intentionally slimy, sticky, or mushy, these are usually not desirable textures. You can check the texture of the food by touching it, as well as gauging it by mouth feel. Keep in mind, however, that just because something feels unusual does not necessarily mean that it has gone bad.

**Discard your ferment if you feel:**
• Slimy textures (if unexpected)

# VEGETABLES AND FRUITS

When people think of fermented vegetables, they typically think of dishes such as sauerkraut or kimchi. But did you know that tea leaves can be fermented? Or plums? This chapter will teach you some universal recipes you may have heard of, and a few new ones that you've probably never tried before.

This classic cucumber pickle has a delicious, zesty flavour. The salt aids the preservation process and helps to maintain the cucumber's crunch.

**Ferment** Bacterial    **Prep** 15 minutes    **Time** 3 to 5 days    **Makes** approx 700g (1½lb)

# PICKLING

Jordanian cucumbers are perfect for pickling due to their small size, thin skin, and lack of seeds. If you can't find Jordanian cucumbers, other varieties will also work well. You can also experiment with different herb and spice additions to create your own unique pickles. Dill, coriander, or mustard seeds are all flavourful additions.

## YOU WILL NEED...

6–8 Jordanian pickling cucumbers

20 black peppercorns

4 cloves garlic, peeled and sliced

2 bay leaves

4 tsp salt

225ml (8fl oz) water

1 litre (1¾ pint) preserving jar

## METHOD

**1** Slice the cucumbers into halves or spears (make sure they don't exceed the height of your jar in length).

White, green, or red peppercorns can also be used.

Cornichon and Kirby cucumbers also pickle well. Wash the cucumbers thoroughly and then rub the skin of each cucumber with a cloth to dry and remove its fine down.

The salt will settle to the bottom.

**2** Place the peppercorns, garlic, and bay leaves in the bottom of a sterilized glass jar. Pack the cucumber spears tightly into the jar, leaving 2.5cm (1in) of headspace. Sprinkle salt over the cucumbers.

**3** Add enough water to completely submerge the cucumbers.

**4** Screw on the lid. Leave at room temperature away from direct sunlight for 1 week, when the pickles should be tender and permeated with brine. Some colour change is normal. Pickles will keep, refrigerated, for up to 3 months.

This is one of the most practical and adaptable pickling techniques you can use. This version calls for carrots, onions, and celery, along with cumin, coriander, and peppercorns, but you can vary the vegetables and spices to suit your tastes.

**Ferment** Bacterial    **Prep** 5 minutes    **Time** 24 to 36 hours    **Makes** approx 700g (1½lb)

# CONTINUOUS PICKLE

##  YOU WiLL NEED...

2 medium carrots, peeled

3 stalks celery

1 medium onion

2 tsp cumin seed

2 tsp coriander seed

1 tsp black peppercorns

225–450ml (1–2 cups) apple cider vinegar or lemon juice

1 tbsp salt

1 litre (1¾ pint) preserving jar

##  METHOD

**1** Chop the carrots and celery into large chunks or sticks. Slice the onion into eighths.

**2** Place cumin, coriander, and peppercorns in the bottom of the sterilized glass jar. Pack the vegetables into the jar and sprinkle with salt. Add vinegar or lemon juice to cover.

**3** Screw the lid on tightly and refrigerate. Depending on how thick the vegetables are, they could be ready to eat within a day.

**4** When the pickles run low, simply add more cut vegetables to the jar. Top off with more vinegar or lemon juice as necessary.

After several rounds of pickling, the brine will become **well marinated** and **flavourful**. You can **bottle the brine** and use it as a tangy seasoning on rice, salads, or grilled vegetables.

This recipe involves a technique common in Indian pickling called tempering: spices are quickly roasted in hot oil to release their flavour and aroma before they are added to the pickling jar.

**Ferment** Bacterial   **Prep** 15 minutes   **Time** 1 to 2 weeks   **Makes** approx 700g (1½lb)

# TURMERIC & CARROT
## PICKLES

 ## YOU WiLL NEED...

1 tsp coconut oil

2 tsp coriander seeds

1 tsp black mustard seeds

1 tsp black peppercorns

8–10 fresh curry leaves
(if available)

2 or 3 carrots, cut into sticks

3 or 4 pieces fresh turmeric root,
cut into wedges

350g (2 cups) cauliflower florets

1 (2.5–5cm; 1–2-in) piece fresh
ginger, peeled and thinly sliced

5 cloves garlic, whole or sliced

1 or 2 Thai chillies (optional)

1 tbsp salt

225–450ml (8–15fl oz) lemon juice

1 litre (1¾ pint) preserving jar

## METHOD

**1** Heat the coconut oil over a high heat in a small frying pan. Add the coriander and black mustard seeds, and peppercorns. After about 1 minute, when the spices begin to release their aroma, add the curry leaves (if using). Stir the spices a few times and remove from heat.

**2** Transfer the tempered spices to the sterilized glass jar. Pack the carrots, turmeric root, cauliflower, ginger, garlic, and chillies (if using) tightly into the jar.

**3** Sprinkle salt over the vegetables and then add enough lemon juice to cover.

**4** Screw the lid on tightly and leave at room temperature, away from light, for 1 to 2 weeks before eating. Pickles will keep, refrigerated, for several months.

*If you can find it, use white turmeric instead of yellow. White turmeric shares some flavour notes with its yellow cousin, but also has notes of mango and ginger.*

Preserved lemons have a bold combination of salty, sour, and bitter flavours. They make an excellent accompaniment to braised meat dishes or a flavourful addition to grain salads.

**Ferment** Bacterial    **Prep** 15 minutes    **Time** 2 to 4 weeks    **Makes** approx 350g (12oz)

# EGYPTIAN PRESERVED LEMON

In Egypt, this ferment is often made with key lime, which has a thin skin and pickles very nicely. Large yellow lemons are used in Morocco and added, along with green olives, to chicken tagine. Preserved lemons can be quite salty and sour, so cut them into smaller, more manageable pieces when serving on their own.

##  YOU WiLL NEED...

4 to 5 medium lemons (preferably a thin-skinned variety)

75g (2½oz) salt

1 tbsp nigella seeds (black seeds)

10 saffron threads or 20 safflower threads

500ml (1 pint) preserving jar

##  METHOD

1 Starting from the stem end, slice the lemons into quarters, leaving the end of each lemon intact.

2 In a small bowl, combine the salt, nigella seeds, and saffron. Over a bowl, liberally spread the salt and spice mix on all exposed surfaces of the lemons.

3 Pack the lemons tightly into the sterilized jar, pressing down to aid in releasing the juices.

4 Sprinkle any remaining salt mix on top and screw the lid on tightly. Store at room temperature, away from direct sunlight, for at least 2 weeks.

5 Refrigerate after opening. Preserved lemons will keep, refrigerated, for several months.

Lift is a tangy and toothsome pickle with a full-bodied texture. One small beet spear is added to infuse the turnips with a beautiful bright fuchsia colour.

**Ferment** Bacterial    **Prep** 15 minutes    **Time** 1 to 2 weeks    **Makes** approx 700g (1½lb)

# LIFT (EGYPTIAN PICKLED TURNIPS)

Pickled turnips are a common addition to shawarma and falafel sandwiches across the Middle East. Egyptian falafel, known as *taameyya*, is made with fava beans instead of chickpeas. Try garnishing a fava bean salad or cooked fava beans with your homemade lift to give it an authentic twist.

 ## YOU WiLL NEED...

1 to 2 medium turnips, sliced into small spears

1 small beetroot, sliced into small spears

2 tbsp salt

225ml (8fl oz) apple cider vinegar

225ml (8fl oz) water

1 litre (1¾ pint) preserving jar

 ## METHOD

**1** Cut off the stem end of 1 turnip and set aside.

**2** Slice the turnips into uniform spears and pack tightly into the sterilized jar along with a small slice of beet.

**3** Add salt, raw apple cider vinegar, and water until the brine level is above the turnips.

**4** Wedge the stem end of the turnip into the jar so that it holds the spears below the brine. Screw the lid on tightly.

**5** Leave to sit at room temperature, out of direct sunlight, for 1 to 2 weeks. At this point, the lift should be ready to eat. It will keep, refrigerated, for several months.

# BASIC KNIFE TECHNIQUES

A good chef's knife is one of the most useful and versatile tools to have in your kitchen. With this simple blade, you can prepare vegetables for just about any type of ferment.

### ⬇ FINE DICE

A small dice creates cubes about 6mm (¼in) on all sides. Firstly, cut your ingredient lengthwise into 6mm (¼in) slabs, stack the slabs and cut into 6mm (¼in) strips, then cut the strips at 6mm (¼in) intervals into cubes.

### ⬆ MEDIUM DICE

A medium dice creates cubes about 1.25cm (½in) on all sides. Firstly, cut your ingredient lengthwise into 1.25cm (½in) slabs, then stack the slabs, cut into 1.25cm (½in) strips, and cut the strips at 1.25cm (½in) intervals into cubes.

## ⬆ PASTE

To make a garlic paste, trim and peel the garlic, slice it finely, and then chop. Bring near the edge of the cutting board and add a small amount of salt. Lay the knife on top of the garlic, parallel to the cutting board, and use the blade to mash the garlic into the cutting board.

## ⬆ MINCE

Finer than a dice, but not quite a paste, a mince works well for herbs as well as vegetables. Chop finely and then continue to chop in a side-to-side motion until you achieve a fine, even texture.

Always work with **high-quality knives** that are **sharp, well-balanced, and suitably sized** for the job. As a general rule, a **chef's knife** will handle any of these techniques with relative ease.

## ⬅ COARSE CHOP

Many ferments call for leafy greens like pak choi or napa cabbage to be coarsely chopped. Cut perpendicular to the stem in 1.25–5cm (½–2-in) pieces.

This quick pickle is often served as an appetizer and palate cleanser in sushi restaurants. The crisp cucumber and toasted sesame seeds make it a great addition to any fish-based meal.

**Ferment** Bacterial    **Prep** 20 minutes    **Time** 30 to 60 minutes    **Makes** approx 350g (12oz)

# SUNOMONO (JAPANESE PICKLED CUCUMBER)

Ginger incorporates best into marinades and dressings when grated very finely. To grate, peel the ginger by scraping the skin off with the edge of a spoon held at a 45-degree angle. Once the ginger is peeled, use a Microplane grater to get the finest results.

## YOU WiLL NEED...

4 to 5 Jordanian cucumbers, finely sliced

½ tsp salt

2 tbsp wakame seaweed flakes

60ml (2fl oz) rice wine vinegar

1 tsp sugar

½ tsp tamari or soy sauce

2 tsp fresh ginger, peeled and finely grated

1 tbsp sesame seeds, toasted

1 tbsp toasted sesame oil

## METHOD

1 In a medium bowl, combine the cucumbers and salt. Set aside to extract some of the moisture for 5 to 10 minutes.

2 In a small bowl, combine the wakame seaweed with a splash of filtered or spring water to rehydrate.

3 In a medium bowl, combine the rice wine vinegar, sugar, tamari, and ginger to make a brine. Stir until the sugar is dissolved.

4 Squeeze the cucumber slices to force out as much liquid as possible. Discard the liquid.

5 Add the cucumber and rehydrated wakame to the brine and mix well. Marinate at room temperature for 30 to 60 minutes.

6 Just before serving, dress with toasted sesame seeds and toasted sesame oil. Refrigerate the leftovers in an airtight container for up to 4 days.

This potent medicinal pickle is made with the unripe ume plum. Serve these strongly salty, aromatic gems with rice or as part of ochazuke, a dish made with rice, green tea, seaweed, and green onions.

**Ferment** Bacterial     **Prep** 5 minutes     **Time** 1 to 2 months     **Makes** approx 700g (1½lb)

# UMEBOSHI (PICKLED UME PLUM)

This recipe calls for sun-drying, so plan to make it when you'll have several days of very hot, breezy sunshine (32°C/90°F). If unripe ume plums are unavailable, use unripe apricots instead.

## ⬇ YOU WiLL NEED...

450g (1lb) unripe ume plums or apricots

60g (2oz) salt

60ml (2fl oz) neutral alcohol, such as vodka or Japanese shochu

5 to 10 Japanese red shiso (perilla) leaves (optional)

1 litre (1¾ pint) preserving jar

## ⬇ METHOD

1 Remove the stems from the ume, using a toothpick if needed. Place in a medium bowl and cover with water. Soak for 8 to 10 hours or overnight.

2 Drain the water and rinse the ume with the alcohol to reduce any chance of mould.

3 Pack the ume in the sterilized jar, adding a layer of salt between each layer. Screw the lid on tightly and leave to sit at room temperature for 3 weeks.

4 After 3 weeks, remove the ume, reserving the brine. Spread the ume in a single layer on a drying tray, cover with muslin to keep off insects, and dry in the sun for 3 days (bring inside at night).

5 Once the ume have shrivelled and the salt has begun to come to the surface (you will see a thin white salt crust), return to the jar with the red shiso (if using) and the reserved pickling brine.

6 Cover tightly with the lid and age for another 3 to 4 weeks at room temperature. For a refined umeboshi, age for 1 to 3 years.

Extend the life of ageing garlic and take advantage of its concentrated flavour by pickling it. Pickled garlic is a welcome addition to any pickle plate or salad.

**Ferment** Bacterial    **Prep** 10 minutes    **Time** 2 to 3 weeks    **Makes** approx 700g (1½lb)

# PICKLED GARLIC

## YOU WILL NEED...

6 heads of garlic, peeled

1 tbsp salt

450–600ml (15fl oz–1 pint) lemon juice

1 litre (1¾ pint) preserving jar

## METHOD

**1** Pack the garlic cloves tightly into the sterilized preserving jar.

**2** Sprinkle salt over the surface of the garlic. Add enough lemon juice to cover.

**3** Screw the lid on tightly and leave to sit at room temperature, out of direct sunlight, for at least 2 weeks.

**4** After 2 weeks, taste the garlic. It can be eaten directly out of the jar and should have a mild, well-rounded flavour.

**5** Store in the pantry instead of the fridge to allow the flavours to continue developing. Pickled garlic will keep for several months.

Pickled garlic can be **cooked or used raw**. It's a great addition to stir-fried dishes, baked vegetables, braised meats, and salads. For brightly coloured garlic, **add turmeric or beetroot juice** to the jar.

Pickling mellows ginger's spicy bite and adds a tangy sweetness. The delicate slices are often served as a palate-cleansing accompaniment to sushi.

| **Ferment** Bacterial | **Prep** 40 minutes | **Time** 1 to 2 weeks | **Makes** approx 350g (12oz) |
| --- | --- | --- | --- |

# PICKLED GINGER

 ## YOU WiLL NEED...

450g (1 lb) fresh root ginger

4 litres (7 pints) water

½ tbsp salt

2 tbsp honey

225ml (7fl oz) rice wine vinegar

500ml (1 pint) jar

 ## METHOD

**1** Peel the ginger by scraping the skin off with the side of a metal spoon. Slice it very thinly with a peeler, mandolin, or sharp knife.

**2** In a saucepan, combine the ginger and 2 litres (3½ pints) of water. Bring to a boil over high heat and boil for 20 minutes. Strain and return the ginger to the pot. Reserve the boiling water for another use if you like (see below).

**3** Add the remaining 2 litres (3½ pints) of water to the pot with the ginger and bring to a boil. Boil for another 20 minutes. Strain the ginger and place in the sterilized jar. Again, reserve this boiling water too if you wish.

**4** In a small bowl, combine the salt, honey, and rice wine vinegar. Stir until the honey and salt are dissolved. Pour it over the ginger in the jar until the ginger is covered. Press down to push out all air bubbles.

**5** Seal the jar and leave to sit at room temperature, away from sunlight, for 1 to 2 weeks. Pickled ginger keeps, refrigerated, for several months.

The reserved boiling water can be drunk as a **powerful ginger tea**, used instead of water to cook ginger rice, or **fermented with sugar and yeast** to make your own ginger beer.

Sauerkraut translates as "sour cabbage" in German, but the flavour is also earthy, salty, and unique. Use the juice from plain sauerkraut to start other lacto-ferments.

**Ferment** Bacterial   **Prep** 40 minutes   **Time** 5+ days   **Makes** approx 2kg (4½lb)

# SAUERKRAUT

You can use any kind of cabbage as the base of your sauerkraut. Green, purple, red, Chinese leaves, and Savoy cabbages will all make delicious sauerkraut. You can also add other vegetables, herbs, and spices. Just stay away from anything too starchy, such as potatoes and yams, which can create slimy textures and off-flavours.

## YOU WiLL NEED...

1 medium head cabbage

1 tbsp salt

2 litre (3½ pint) preserving jar

## METHOD

**1** Remove one whole outer cabbage leaf and set it aside. Cut the cabbage in half and remove the core. Slice into fine ribbons, about 6mm (¼in) wide.

Try adding shredded **carrots**, whole **garlic, jalapeños, apples,** or **onions** to your kraut. The preparation of each ingredient will affect the **flavour and texture** of the finished product.

Set aside a whole cabbage leaf to cover the sauerkraut later.

**2** In a medium bowl, combine cabbage and salt and mix well to distribute the salt evenly.

**3** With your hands, massage the cabbage shreds, mashing and squeezing them until the cabbage releases a significant amount of liquid.

**4** Transfer the mixture to the sterilized preserving jar and press down until the cabbage sits below the surface of the liquid.

**Vegetables must be below the liquid line to prevent spoilage.**

Continued ⇨

**5** Insert the reserverd whole cabbage leaf into the mouth of the jar and tuck it around the mixture to keep any small bits from floating to the surface.

Sauerkraut, like any fermented food, will have a strong, distinctive smell that is not at all unpleasant. If your kraut develops a (sulphur) smell that is distinctly rotten, discard your ferment.

Some discolouration near the surface is normal. Simply scrape off and discard.

**6** Place a small jar upside down on top of the whole cabbage leaf and press down firmly (this keeps the mixture submerged). Screw the lid tightly on the large jar, then release the lid with a one-eighth turn to allow gases to escape during the fermentation process.

**7** Set the jar on a plate and place out of direct sunlight. Allow to ferment at room temperature for at least 5 days. Refrigerate once you are satisfied with the level of fermentation.

Krauts can be **aged for months and even years.** If you like a stronger-flavoured kraut with more zing, consider a longer ferment time.

**A plate will catch any overflow of juices.**

Kelp and nori bring the briny flavour of the ocean to this probiotic powerhouse, as well as essential nutrients such as calcium and iodine.

**Ferment** Bacterial    **Prep** 40 minutes    **Ferment** 5+ days    **Makes** approx 2kg (4½lb)

# SEAWEED KRAUT

##  YOU WiLL NEED...

1 medium head cabbage, sliced into 6mm (¼in) ribbons

½ tbsp salt

6 to 7 dried kelp fronds, crumbled

30g (1oz) dried nori seaweed, crumbled

2 litre (3½ pint) preserving jar

*Experiment with different kinds and combinations of seaweeds.* **Dulse, kelp, nori, kombu, wakame,** *or* **spirulina** *will each lend different flavours and nutritional benefits to your kraut.*

##  METHOD

**1** In a large bowl, combine the cabbage and salt. Cover with a plate and set aside to extract some of the moisture for 1 to 3 hours.

**2** Add the kelp and nori to the cabbage. With clean hands, mix the seaweed and cabbage thoroughly, massaging them to release liquid.

**3** Transfer the mixture to the sterilized jar and press it down until all the ingredients sit below the surface of the liquid.

**4** Screw on the lid tightly and place out of direct sunlight. Allow to ferment at room temperature for at least 5 days.

**5** Refrigerate once you are satisfied with the level of fermentation. Kraut will keep for several months in the fridge.

This Indian-inspired spiced kraut is bursting with aromatic and savoury flavours. You can keep spices whole or grind them, depending on your preference.

**Ferment** Bacterial    **Prep time** 45 minutes    **Ferment time** 5 days    **Makes** approx 2kg (4½lb)

# MASALA KRAUT

##  YOU WiLL NEED...

1 medium head cabbage, sliced into 6mm (¼in) ribbons

1 tbsp salt

1 small onion, finely chopped

3.75cm (1½in) piece fresh root ginger, peeled and grated

1 tsp coriander seeds

12 to 15 curry leaves, finely chopped

2 tsp black mustard seeds

1 tsp cumin seeds

1 tsp turmeric

1 tsp fenugreek

¼ tsp asafoetida powder

1 tsp cayenne pepper (optional)

2 litre (3½ pint) preserving jar

## METHOD

1 In a large bowl, combine the cabbage and salt. Cover with a plate and set aside for 1 to 3 hours .

2 Add the onion and ginger to the chopped cabbage and mix well to combine.

3 Add the coriander seeds, curry leaves, black mustard seeds, cumin seeds, turmeric, fenugreek, and asafoetida to the cabbage mixture. With clean hands, mix and massage them thoroughly. Add cayenne (if using) and mix in well with a spoon.

4 Transfer the mixture to the sterilized jar and press down until all the ingredients sit below the surface of the liquid.

5 Screw on the lid tightly and place out of direct sunlight. Allow to ferment at room temperature for at least 5 days.

6 Refrigerate once you are satisfied with the level of fermentation. Kraut will keep for several months in the fridge.

**Asafoetida powder** is derived from a species of **fennel** and is a common ingredient in **Indian vegetarian cuisine**. It can be purchased at Indian grocery shops or speciality spice stores.

This kraut made with all root vegetables is tangy and toothsome. For textural and visual variety, process your root vegetables using several different techniques, such as slicing, grating, and chopping.

**Ferment** Bacterial   **Prep** 40 minutes   **Time** 5+ days   **Makes** approx 1kg (2¼lb)

# ROOT KRAUT

This kraut technique works well with a wide variety of root vegetables. Try experimenting with carrot, radish, kohlrabi, horseradish, ginger, turmeric, onions, and garlic. Just avoid starchy roots such as potato and yam, which require special care and techniques to ferment.

 ## YOU WILL NEED...

- 1 large yellow beetroot, sliced, grated, or chopped
- 1 medium turnip, sliced, grated, or chopped
- 1 small swede, sliced, grated, or chopped
- 2 parsnips, sliced, grated, or chopped
- ¼ bulb celeriac, sliced, grated, or chopped
- 1 tbsp green peppercorns
- 1 tbsp salt
- 2 litre (3½ pint) preserving jar

 ## METHOD

**1** In a large bowl, combine the beetroot, turnip, swede, parsnips, celeriac, green peppercorns, and salt. Cover with a plate and set aside to extract some of the moisture for 1 to 3 hours.

**2** With your hands, mix thoroughly and massage to release more of the liquid.

**3** Transfer the mixture to the sterilized jar and press down until all the ingredients sit below the surface of the liquid.

**4** Screw on the lid tightly and place out of direct sunlight. Allow to ferment at room temperature for at least 5 days.

**5** Refrigerate once you are satisfied with the level of fermentation. Kraut will keep for several months in the fridge.

This cabbage pickle is a common side dish in El Salvador. Its vinegary tang and crunchy texture will bring brightness and flavour to sandwiches or long-simmered meat dishes.

**Ferment** Bacterial     **Prep** 40 minutes     **Time** 1 day     **Makes** approx 2kg (4½lb)

# CURTIDO

Green cabbage and white onion are most often used to make curtido, but you could also use red cabbage and red onion in this recipe for a vibrant, fuchsia-hued ferment.

Curtido is **traditionally served** along with red salsa on top of pupusas – **thick Salvadorian tortillas** that are stuffed with cheese, beans, vegetables, or meat.

##  YOU WILL NEED...

1 medium head cabbage, sliced into 6mm (¼ in) ribbons

2 carrots, peeled and grated

1 small onion, thinly sliced

1 tbsp dried oregano

100ml (3½fl oz) apple cider vinegar

1 tbsp salt

2 jalapeños, thinly sliced (optional)

1 tsp cayenne pepper (optional)

2 litre (3½ pint) preserving jar

## METHOD

1 In a large bowl, combine the cabbage, carrots, onion, oregano, vinegar, and salt. Cover with a plate and leave for 1 hour at room temperature.

2 With your hands, mix thoroughly and massage the ingredients to release their liquid. Add the jalapeños (if using) and cayenne (if using).

3 Transfer the mixture to the sterilized jar and press down until all the ingredients sit below the surface of the liquid.

4 Screw on the lid and then loosen it slightly with one-eighth of a turn. Place out of direct sunlight and ferment at room temperature for at least 1 day.

5 Refrigerate once you are satisfied with the level of fermentation. Curtido will keep, refrigerated, for several months.

Kimchi is a spicy fermented dish from Korea that can be made with a variety of ingredients. This basic version is fresh, pungent, and flavourful.

**Ferment** Bacterial/Yeast **Prep** 3 hours **Time** 1 to 2 weeks **Makes** approx 2kg (4½lb)

# KIMCHI

Kimchi benefits from a lower fermentation temperature (below 27°C/80°F) and a few weeks of ageing. Even if your batch tastes bland after the week-long ferment, it may blossom after a month of ageing in the fridge.

 **YOU WiLL NEED...**

1 medium head Chinese leaves

50g (1¾oz) salt

1 medium daikon radish

1 ripe pear

½ white onion

7.5cm (3 in) piece fresh root ginger

5 cloves garlic

60g (2oz) Korean red pepper powder (gochugaru)

1 tsp Thai fish sauce (nam pla) (optional)

5 to 7 spring onions, finely chopped

Cutting the leaves into quarters makes it easier to distribute the seasonings.

 **METHOD**

**1** Cut the leaves into quarters and remove the inner stem, keeping the leaves intact.

**2** Generously distribute salt between the leaves, working it all the way down to the core. Place the cabbage leaves in a shallow bowl and leave them at room temperature for 2 to 6 hours.

Korean red pepper powder is a coarsely ground red pepper with a texture between a flake and a powder. It can be found online and in speciality spice shops.

**3** In a food processor fitted with a chopping blade, purée the radish, pear, white onion, ginger, garlic, Korean red pepper powder, and fish sauce (if using) into a smooth paste.

Garlic cloves can be added whole to the food processor.

Continued

**4** Rinse the salt from between each of the leaves, then squeeze them to drain as much of the water as possible.

In Korea, kimchi is often made with **vegetables that are in season**, and **isn't limited to cabbage** as the main ingredient. Try using cucumber, cubed daikon radish, or pak choi in place of cabbage.

**Try to distribute the paste on the Chinese leaves as evenly as possible.**

**5** Spread the paste and chopped spring onions onto all the leaves, making sure to cover them all the way down to the core.

**6** Pack the seasoned Chinese leaf quarters into a 2 litre (3½ pint) sterilized preserving jar and press down to release trapped air. Spread any remaining paste on the surface of the cabbage. Screw on the lid tightly, then loosen it again slightly with a one-eighth turn.

Loosening the lid slightly allows gases to escape.

Check your kimchi often to ensure that no mould forms on the surface of the ferment.

Kimchi is an **incredibly versatile condiment**. It's delicious eaten on its own, but it's also a flavourful addition to eggs, stir-fried dishes, soups, and salads. Some people prefer it to sauerkraut.

Fermenting will soften the vegetables and deepen the spice flavours.

**7** Place out of direct sunlight and ferment at room temperature for 1 to 2 weeks. Once you are satisfied with the level of fermentation, refrigerate and chop to serve. Kimchi will keep, refrigerated, several months.

This twist on kimchi replaces the traditional Chinese leaves with pak choi and uses green chillies instead of red chillie paste for a lighter colour and milder flavour.

**Ferment** Bacterial/Yeast  **Prep** 3 hours  **Time** 1 to 2 weeks  **Makes** approx 2kg (4½lb)

# PAK CHOI
# WHITE KIMCHI

Pak choi is just one of the greens that can stand in for cabbage in kimchi. Try experimenting with other leafy greens such as kale, collard, baby pak choi, and chard. Bear in mind that tender greens ferment faster than sturdy ones.

## YOU WiLL NEED...

1kg (2 lb) pak choi, cut into quarters

1 small daikon radish, shredded or sliced

3 tbsp salt

½ ripe pear, cored

½ white onion

5cm (2-in) piece fresh ginger, peeled

2 cloves garlic

3 or 4 green chillies, such as jalapeño or serrano, stems and seeds removed

½ tsp Thai fish sauce (nam pla) (optional)

3 or 4 spring onions, white and green parts, finely chopped

½ bunch fresh coriander, stems and leaves, finely chopped

2 litre (3½ pint) preserving jar

## METHOD

1 In a large bowl, combine the pak choi and radish. Sprinkle with salt and allow to sit at room temperature for 1 to 3 hours.

2 In a food processor, purée the pear, onion, ginger, garlic, chillies, and fish sauce (if using) into a smooth paste.

3 Rinse the salt from the pak choi and daikon and squeeze out as much water as possible.

4 Spread the paste, chopped spring onion, and coriander all over the pak choi and daikon radish.

5 Pack seasoned pak choi and daikon into the sterilized jar and press down to release any trapped air. Spread any remaining paste on the surface of the vegetables.

6 Screw on the lid and loosen again with a one-eighth turn. Ferment at room temperature, away from direct sunlight, for 1 to 2 weeks.

7 Once you are satisfied with the level of fermentation, refrigerate and chop to serve. Kimchi will keep, refrigerated, for several months.

# SLICING, PEELING, & GRATING TECHNIQUES

When preparing a large batch of vegetables for fermentation, the right tool can save time and create shapes and sizes that may be hard or impossible to achieve with a knife. Here are some handy tools and the results they produce.

### ◁ ZEST

The small, sharp holes of a rasp-style grater, such as a Microplane, are perfect for zesting citrus fruits. They can also be used to create a paste-like consistency out of ginger, radish, and onion.

The techniques you use can impact **the taste and textures** of your ferments. Experiment with **different shapes and sizes** of ingredients to see what best suits your tastes.

### ▷ FINE GRATE

Use a fine grater to grate tough, fibrous roots and vegetables. This will allow them to break down more easily during fermentation.

## ⬆ COARSE GRATE

Vegetables that are coarsely grated will add a unique texture to your ferments and won't lose their shape as quickly as items that have been finely grated.

## ⬆ RIBBONS

A peeler isn't just for removing the outer skin, you can also use it to make ribbons. Depending on the length of your peeler, you can achieve long, thin strips that are 2.5–5cm (1–2in) wide.

## ⬇ JULIENNE

Use a zigzag peeler to create thin, julienned strips quickly and easily. It works like a regular peeler and can be found in speciality cookware stores and onlilne.

## ⬇ THIN SLICES

Use a mandolin to achieve very thin, even slices. Some models can be adjusted for varying thicknesses and may have attachments for julienne or waffle cuts.

The flavour of these tangy and juicy tomatoes deepens and intensifies over time. Try them as a refreshing side dish with grilled meats or served on top of a salad.

**Ferment** Bacterial    **Prep** 15 minutes    **Time** 1 to 3 days    **Makes** approx 900g (2lb)

# PICKLED TOMATOES

## ⬇ YOU WILL NEED...

5 to 6 tomatoes

5 cloves garlic

50g (1¾oz) celery leaves, finely chopped

2 tsp salt

4 tbsp apple cider vinegar

> **After 5 or 6 days in the fridge,** these tomatoes can get a bit mushy. That's the perfect time to **use them for gazpacho, tomato sauce,** or **salsa**. Just blend them up and use as a tomato base.

## ⬇ METHOD

**1** Cut the tomatoes into 1.25cm (½-in) slices, perpendicular to the core.

**2** With a pestle and mortar or the blade of a chef's knife, make a paste out of the garlic. Mix in the salt and celery leaf. Spread the paste over the cut surfaces of the tomatoes.

**3** In a medium glass or ceramic dish, layer the tomatoes on top of each other, dressing each layer with 1 tablespoon of the apple cider vinegar.

**4** Cover and leave to sit at room temperature for at least 6 hours. If pickling for more than 6 hours, transfer to fridge. Use within a week.

This delightfully toothsome pickled aubergine has a deep and balanced flavour. Its tangy flavour is an excellent complement to rich dishes, especially red meats and grilled vegetables.

**Ferment** Bacterial    **Prep** 45 minutes    **Time** 1 to 3 days    **Makes** 8 to 10 aubergines

# PICKLED AUBERGINE

## YOU WiLL NEED...

8 to 10 small finger aubergines

8 cloves garlic

1 small bunch parsley, leaves and stems, finely chopped

1 tbsp salt

120ml (4fl oz) apple cider vinegar

## METHOD

**1** In a saucepan with a steaming basket or a food steamer, steam the aubergines whole for 20 to 30 minutes until tender, but not soggy.

**2** With a pestle and mortar or the blade of a chef's knife, make a paste out of the garlic. Mix in the parsley and salt.

**3** Remove the stems from the aubergines and cut a slit down the length of each one, making sure not to cut all the way through. (They should look like little aubergine canoes.)

**4** Spread 2 to 3 teaspoons of garlic and parsley paste into each aubergine. Stack the aubergines in a medium glass or ceramic dish and spread any remaining paste on top. Pour enough apple cider vinegar over the aubergines to submerge them.

**5** Cover and refrigerate. Leave to sit for at least 1 day before eating. Aubergines will keep, refrigerated, for 1 to 2 weeks.

For a **less sharp pickle, use equal parts vinegar and water.** Diluting the vinegar will shorten the life of the pickle, but it will still keep for at least a week.

This unique ferment has a pungent, bittersweet flavour and is considered a digestive aid. It's a great way to make use of the used tea leaves left over after brewing Chinese or Japanese tea.

**Ferment** Bacterial     **Prep** 10 minutes     **Time** 4 to 6 days     **Makes** approx 75g (2½oz)

# LAHPET (BURMESE PICKLED TEA LEAVES)

In the traditional Burmese dish *lahpet thoke*, lahpet is served on a bed of shredded cabbage and surrounded by piles of fried garlic, fried butter beans, roasted peanuts, toasted sesame seeds, tomatoes, green chillies, dried shrimps, fried shredded coconut, and fried ginger slices. It is dressed with lime juice, sesame or peanut oil, and Thai fish sauce.

## YOU WiLL NEED...

75g (2½oz) used whole tea leaves (green, white, or oolong)

1 tsp salt

2 tbsp lime or lemon juice

240ml (8oz) jar

## METHOD

1 Remove the large stems from the tea leaves and finely chop the leaves. In a small bowl, combine the chopped tea leaves, salt, and lemon juice and mix together thoroughly.

2 Pack the mixture into the sterilized jar and cover tightly with the lid.

3 Leave to ferment at room temperature, away from sunlight, for 4 to 6 days.

4 When your are satisfied with the level of fermentation, transfer to the fridge. Lahpet will keep, refrigerated, for several months.

Lahpet is popular in Myanmar, where it is considered **a national delicacy** and prized for its **medicinal properties**. In addition to aiding digestion, it is also a **mild stimulant** and can be used to ward off sleepiness.

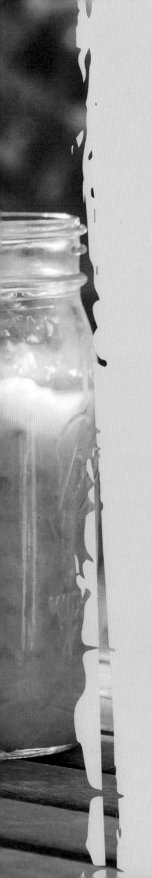

# CONDIMENTS

Some of the most ubiquitous condiments in the world –
mustard, ketchup, chutney, hot sauce – take on new life
and flavour when they're fermented. This chapter
introduces you to some amazing (and healthful)
fermented condiments that can add a new dimension
of taste to everyday foods.

This fermented ketchup has the familiar tanginess of store-bought varieties, but without the high-fructose corn syrup and preservatives. Its robust flavour is a welcome addition to burgers, chips, meatloaf, or hot dogs.

**Ferment** Bacterial/Yeast    **Prep** 10 minutes    **Time** 2 to 3 days    **Makes** approx 200ml (7fl oz)

# KETCHUP

You can use any liquid probiotic starter for this recipe, but the final flavour will be affected by which one you choose. Sauerkraut juice or a basic water kefir, such as plain coconut water kefir, are recommended for this recipe.

 ## YOU WILL NEED...

175ml (6oz) tomato paste

2 tbsp "starter" liquid (sauerkraut juice, water kefir, or whey)

1 tbsp maple syrup or honey

1 clove garlic, minced to a paste

¼ tsp salt

⅛ tsp ground cinnamon

A pinch of ground cloves

A pinch of cayenne pepper

2 tbsp apple cider vinegar

500ml (1 pint) preserving jar

## METHOD

**1** Combine the tomato paste, starter liquid, maple syrup or honey, garlic, salt, cinnamon, cloves, and cayenne pepper in the sterilized jar and mix well.

**2** Pour the apple cider vinegar onto the surface of the ketchup. This will help to inhibit the growth of mould on the surface.

**3** Cover tightly with a lid and leave to sit at room temperature, away from light, for 2 to 3 days.

**4** When you are satisfied with the level of fermentation, mix the vinegar on the surface into the ketchup. For a thinner ketchup, mix in more starter liquid, vinegar, or water. The ketchup will keep for 1 to 2 weeks in the fridge.

Mole is a sauce from southern Mexico that has many variations and applications. This recipe brings the spicy, smoky, and earthy flavours of mole rojo to ketchup.

**Ferment** Bacterial/Yeast    **Prep** 10 minutes    **Time** 2 to 3 days    **Makes** approx 200g (7oz)

# MOLE KETCHUP

## YOU WILL NEED...

175ml (6oz) tomato paste

2 tbsp starter liquid (sauerkraut juice, water kefir, or whey)

1 tbsp maple syrup or honey

1 clove garlic, minced to a paste

¼ tsp salt

¼ tsp ground cinnamon

2 tsp raw cacao powder (or cocoa powder if unavailable)

½ tsp smoked paprika

A pinch of ground cloves

A pinch of cayenne pepper (optional)

3 tbsp apple cider vinegar

500ml (1 pint) preserving jar

## METHOD

**1** Combine the tomato paste, starter liquid, maple syrup or honey, garlic paste, salt, cinnamon, cacao powder, smoked paprika, cloves, and cayenne pepper in the sterilized jar and mix well.

**2** Pour the apple cider vinegar onto the surface of the ketchup. This will help inhibit the growth of mould on the surface.

**3** Cover tightly with a lid and leave to sit at room temperature, away from light, for 2 to 3 days.

**4** When you are satisfied with the level of fermentation, mix the vinegar on the surface into the ketchup and enjoy. Ketchup will keep for 1 to 2 weeks in the fridge.

To make **Chipotle chocolate ketchup,** substitute chipotle chilli powder for the paprika. If the flavour of the cacao is too bitter, add a little more maple syrup or honey.

Homemade horseradish is extra hot, pungent, and medicinal. Use it on sandwiches or as a base for dressings and marinades. A little bit goes a long way!

**Ferment** Bacterial/Yeast    **Prep** 30 minutes    **Time** 7 days    **Makes** approx 250g (9oz)

# HORSERADISH

 ## YOU WiLL NEED...

100g (3½oz) horseradish root (about half a root)

4 tbsp apple cider vinegar

½ tsp salt

500ml (1 pint) preserving jar

 ## METHOD

**1** Peel the horseradish root and cut out any woody parts.

**2** Outside or in a well-ventilated area, grate the horseradish using a Microplane or box grater. (Horseradish can irritate the eyes and nose; use caution and try not to inhale the pungent oils while grating it.)

**3** In a medium bowl, combine the grated horseradish, apple cider vinegar, and salt and mix well.

**4** Transfer to the sterilized jar and cover tightly. Leave to sit at room temperature, away from light, for at least 1 week.

**5** When you are satisfied with the level of fermentation, transfer the jar to the fridge. Horseradish will keep, refrigerated, for several months.

A **food processor** will break down the horseradish root into a **more paste-like consistency**. Blend in 120ml (4fl oz) of water for a slightly **mellower and smoother** horseradish.

This basic mustard recipe is hot and flavourful. With longer ageing, the intense burn will soften and become milder. Serve with grilled meats, spread on sandwiches, or use as a spicy dip.

**Ferment** Bacterial/Yeast    **Prep** 15 minutes    **Time** 2 to 3 days    **Makes** approx 200g (7oz)

# MUSTARD

Yellow mustard seeds tends to be hotter than brown mustard seeds. Try playing with different ratios of the two types of mustard seed to arrive at your preferred level of intensity.

## YOU WiLL NEED...

50g (1¾oz) ground mustard seeds

120ml (4fl oz) water

4 tbsp starter liquid (sauerkraut juice, whey, or water kefir)

1 tbsp honey

½ tsp turmeric

½ tsp salt

2 tbsp apple cider vinegar

500ml (1 pint) preserving jar

## METHOD

1 Combine the mustard seeds, water, starter liquid, honey, turmeric, and salt in the sterilized jar. Mix well.

2 Pour the apple cider vinegar onto the surface of the mustard to inhibit mould growth. Cover the jar tightly with the lid and leave to sit at room temperature, away from light, for 2 to 3 days.

3 When you are satisfied with the level of fermentation, transfer to the fridge and enjoy. Mustard will keep, refrigerated, for several months, and its flavour will continue to mellow over time.

This recipe makes a whole-seed mustard with a coarse texture. **For a smoother mustard** with a more conventional texture, **use mustard powder** instead of ground mustard seed.

# MORE WAYS TO USE CONDIMENTS

When you make fermented condiments, you open the door to a world of possibilities. The condiment recipes in this book can be combined and adapted to create a wide array of dips, toppings, and sauces.

## MUSTARD

**Honey Mustard** Combine mustard and honey in a 2:1 ratio.

**Mustard vinaigrette** Whisk equal parts of olive oil and apple cider vinegar with regular or Dijon mustard. Add salt to taste and honey for sweetness.

## KETCHUP

**Quick pizza sauce** Combine 200g (7oz) of ketchup, 1 fresh tomato (grated), 1 tsp dried oregano, and 2 cloves garlic (paste) and mix well.

**Cocktail sauce** Mix 200g (7oz) of ketchup with 2 tbsp of horseradish, a squirt of lemon juice, 1/2 tsp hot chilli sauce, and ground black pepper to taste.

## CULTURED COCONUT CREAM

**Cake icing** Mix 125g (4½oz) of coconut cream (p88) with 85g (3oz) of honey or maple syrup and a dash of vanilla extract.

**Coconut chocolate pudding** Combine 125g (4½oz) of coconut cream with 1 tbsp of cacao powder and 2 tbsp of honey or maple syrup. Top with nuts or fresh fruit.

## CASHEW SPREAD

**Vegan aioli** Combine 200g (7oz) of cashew spread (p85) with 3 cloves of garlic (paste) and a pinch of salt to taste.

**Creamy avocado dip** Combine 1 mashed avocado with 2 tbsp of cashew spread and salt and cayenne pepper to taste.

## HORSERADISH

**Creamy horseradish salad dressing** Combine 60g (2oz) of sour cream, 2 tbsp of horseradish, 2 tbsp of fresh herbs, salt and pepper to taste.

**Red horseradish** Combine 60g (2oz) of horseradish with 2 tbsp of grated beetroot.

## HOT SAUCE

**Fresh salsa** Combine 2 tomatoes (chopped), ¼ medium onion (diced), a small bunch of fresh coriander (chopped), 2 to 4 tbsp hot pepper sauce, juice of 1 lime, and salt to taste.

**Spicy aioli** Combine 200g (7oz) of cashew spread, 2 to 4 tbsp of hot chilli sauce, 2 cloves of garlic (paste), and a pinch of salt to taste.

**Not just for fries**
Fermented ketchup makes a great base for other condiments and has no added sugar.

Fermented condiments are a much **healthier alternative** to commercially-made condiments, which can contain processed oils, added sugar, emulsifiers, and preservatives.

**Turn Up the Heat!**
Wild Habanero Hot Sauce will bring serious heat to chicken wings, add a peppery kick to eggs, and balance the sweetness of chutneys.

Sauerkraut adds a unique tanginess to this mild mustard, perfect for topping brats or hot dogs. As with all homemade mustards, it will continue to mellow with age.

**Ferment** Bacterial/Yeast    **Prep** 5 minutes    **Time** 2 to 3 days    **Makes** approx 200g (7oz)

# SAUERKRAUT MUSTARD

 ## YOU WiLL NEED...

3 tbsp yellow mustard seeds

120ml (4fl oz) sauerkraut juice

100g (3½oz) sauerkraut

240ml (8fl oz) preserving jar

 ## METHOD

**1** Place the yellow mustard seeds and sauerkraut juice in the sterilized jar. Screw the lid on tightly and leave to sit at room temperature for 2 to 3 days.

**2** In a blender, combine the sauerkraut, mustard seeds, and soaking liquid. Blend until smooth.

**3** Transfer to a small jar and refrigerate. Mustard will keep, refrigerated, for several months.

Different krauts will lend **different characteristics** to this mustard. Try using red cabbage kraut for a **vibrant colour,** or a heavily spiced sauerkraut, such as Masala Kraut, for a **unique flavour.**

The original Dijon mustard was made using the juice of unripe green grapes. Today, white wine gives Dijon mustard its characteristic flavour.

**Ferment** Bacterial    **Prep** 5 minutes    **Time** 2 to 3 days    **Makes** approx 225g (8oz)

# DIJON MUSTARD

##  YOU WiLL NEED...

2 tbsp black mustard seeds

4 tbsp yellow mustard seeds

60ml (2fl oz) sauerkraut juice

60ml (2fl oz) white wine (any variety)

½ tsp salt

500ml (1 pint) preserving jar

##  METHOD

**1** Combine the black and yellow mustard seeds, sauerkraut juice, white wine, and salt in the sterilized jar.

**2** Screw the lid on tightly and leave to sit at room temperature, away from light, for at least 2 to 3 days.

**3** Transfer the contents of the jar to a small blender or food processor and blend to a paste.

**4** Once smooth, transfer the mustard to a small jar and refrigerate. Mustard will keep, refrigerated, for several months.

Add a teaspoon or two of dijon mustard to **homemade vinaigrette dressings.** Mustard is an **emulsifier** and will help the oil and vinegar to **mix thoroughly.**

This hot sauce is creamy and flavourful. A longer fermentation time will yield a thicker, salsa-like texture. Blend more of the brine with the peppers for a thinner hot sauce.

**Ferment** Bacterial    **Prep** 15 minutes    **Time** 1 to 2 Weeks    **Makes** approx 450ml (15fl oz)

# JALAPEÑO HOT SAUCE

The whey and salt brine called for here complements the flavour of the jalapeños, but sauerkraut juice, lemon juice, vinegar, or even a simple salt water brine could also be used. To tone down the heat, incorporate 1 green bell pepper along with the jalapeños. This will keep the colour consistent, add some sweetness, and buffer the spiciness of the jalapeños.

### YOU WiLL NEED...

8 to 10 medium jalapeño peppers

1 tbsp salt

350ml (12fl oz) whey (from yogurt or cheese making)

1 litre (1¾ pint) preserving jar

 **METHOD**

**1** Remove the stems and then quarter the peppers, leaving the stem ends intact.

**2** Pack peppers tightly into a 1-quart (1l) jar, leaving 2.5cm (1in) of headspace.

**3** Distribute the salt evenly over the peppers.

**5** Drain the peppers, reserving the brine. In a food processor, purée the peppers, adding small amounts of reserved brine as needed. When a pourable consistency is reached, transfer to a swing stopper bottle and refrigerate. The sauce will keep for several months.

A funnel is helpful when using swing stopper bottles.

Any **type of hot pepper** can be used for this recipe. If you like a **more gentle sauce**, choose milder peppers as your base. For a **more intense sauce,** consider the habanero or serrano varieties.

**4** Pour the whey over the peppers until they are fully submerged. Seal with the lid and set on a plate (to catch any overflow). Ferment at room temperature, away from light, for 1 to 2 weeks.

This is a sauce for spice lovers! Habaneros bring an intense heat to this colourful sauce. If you prefer a milder flavour, replace some or all of the habaneros with the chillies of your choice.

**Ferment** Bacterial/Yeast    **Prep** 10 minutes    **Time** 1 to 2 weeks    **Makes** approx 450ml (15fl oz)

# WILD HABANERO
# HOT SAUCE

You can reuse the brine from pickling peppers several times, adding complexity and heat to each subsequent batch. You can also use the brine to pickle other vegetables or as part of a marinade. The hot sauce itself is a ferment that deepens and mellows with age.

## 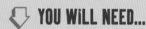 YOU WILL NEED...

12 habanero peppers

2 orange bell peppers

1½ tbsp salt

225–450ml (8–15fl oz) water

1 litre (1¾ pint) preserving jar

## METHOD

1 Remove the habanero stems, slice down the middle, and place in the sterilized jar.

2 Slice the orange bell peppers into large pieces and remove the seeds. Add to the jar with the habaneros, packing tightly.

3 Add salt and enough water to cover the peppers, leaving at least 2.5cm (1in) of headspace to allow for expansion during fermentation.

4 Screw on the lid and then loosen with a one-eighth turn. Place the jar on a small plate or bowl to catch potential overflow and ferment at room temperature, away from light, for 1 to 2 weeks.

5 When you are satisfied with the level of fermentation, pour off and reserve the brine. Transfer the peppers to a food processor. Purée until a pourable hot sauce consistency is reached, adding small amounts of reserved brine as necessary.

6 Transfer to a bottle or jar and refrigerate. The sauce will keep, refrigerated, for several months.

This tangy and delicious spread is reminiscent of mayonnaise in taste and texture, making it an excellent option for those who avoid eggs. Try using it as a dip, as a sandwich spread, or as a base for salad dressing.

**Ferment** Bacterial/Yeast    **Prep** 5 minutes    **Time** 2 days    **Makes** approx 500g (1lb 2oz)

# CASHEW SPREAD

Try experimenting with other nuts in this spread. Cashews will yield the smoothest result in a home blender, but any nut will produce a delicious spread, albeit with a grainier texture.

## YOU WiLL NEED...

115g (4oz) raw, unsalted cashews

180ml (6fl oz) water or **rejuvelac** (p129)

180ml (6fl oz) sauerkraut juice

1 litre (1¾ pint) preserving jar

## METHOD

1 Rinse the cashews and place in the sterilized jar. Add the water and sauerkraut juice, making sure all the cashews are submerged.

2 Screw the lid on tightly and ferment at room temperature, away from light, for 1 to 2 days.

3 In a food processor, combine the cashews and half of the soaking liquid. Blend until creamy, adding more soaking liquid if needed to achieve a spreadable consistency.

4 Transfer to a jar, cover tightly with the lid, and refrigerate 8 to 10 hours or overnight to achieve a thick, creamy texture. The spread will keep, refrigerated, for 3 to 4 weeks.

Roasted onions impart a sweet, caramelized flavour to this tangy spread. Use it to add moisture and flavour to sandwiches, wraps, or grilled meats.

**Ferment** Bacterial     **Prep** 15 minutes     **Time** 2 to 3 days     **Makes** approx 500g (1lb 2oz)

# SWEET ONION RELISH

##  YOU WiLL NEED...

3 to 4 onions, quartered

2 tsp salt

2 tbsp starter liquid (whey, sauerkraut juice, or apple cider vinegar)

Clay is an amazing material with **insulating properties** that allow food to cook deeply and evenly. Try using an **unglazed clay casserole** or **covered pot** to cook the onions for this relish.

## METHOD

**1** Preheat the oven to 180°C (350°F/Gas 4).

**2** Place the onions in a single layer in a medium clay or ceramic baking dish. Cover and roast for 1 hour. The roasted onions should be very soft and darkly caramelized at the edges when ready.

**3** Chop the onions very finely, mix with the starter liquid, and stir to thoroughly combine. Transfer to a jar and cover tightly with the lid.

**4** Ferment at room temperature for 12 to 36 hours before refrigerating. Relish will keep, refrigerated, for up to 1 week.

Chutneys are versatile condiments that can be enjoyed with breads, meats, or cheeses. This sweet-and-sour spiced chutney is delicious on dosa or uttapam.

**Ferment** Bacterial **Prep** 5 minutes **Time** 1 to 3 days **Makes** approx 500g (1lb 2oz)

# TAMARIND DATE CHUTNEY

##  YOU WiLL NEED...

8 large dates, pitted and chopped

115g (4oz) seedless tamarind paste

500ml (16fl oz) water

1 tsp cumin seeds

1 tsp coriander seeds

1 tsp fresh root ginger, grated

½ tsp salt

1 or 2 dried chillies of your choice

2 tbsp starter liquid (whey, apple cider vinegar, or sauerkraut juice)

500ml (1 pint) jar

## METHOD

**1** In a small pan, simmer the dates, tamarind paste, and water for 10 to 15 minutes.

**2** Meanwhile, toast the cumin and coriander seeds and chillies in a dry pan over a medium heat for 1 to 2 minutes or until fragrant. Transfer to a spice grinder or pestle and mortar and grind to a coarse powder.

**3** Add the ground spices, ginger, and salt to the pan and continue to simmer until the dates disintegrate. Add water in small amounts if the mixture begins to get too thick.

**4** Cool the mixture to room temperature and stir in 1 tablespoon of the starter liquid. Transfer to the sterilized jar and add remaining 1 tablespoon of starter liquid to the surface. Cover tightly with the lid.

**5** Ferment at room temperature for 1 to 3 days. Stir well before refrigerating. Chutney will keep, refrigerated, for up to 1 week.

Dates bring a rich sweetness to this chutney, but **other dried fruits could be used** as well for a **completely different flavour.** Just make sure that any dried fruits you use are **unsulphured, unsweetened,** and without **added oil.**

This creamy ferment is an excellent vegan yogurt alternative. Top with berries and granola for a probiotic-rich breakfast, or use as a base for curries.

**Ferment** Bacterial/Yeast    **Prep** 30 minutes    **Time** 1 to 3 days    **Makes** approx 500g (1lb 2oz)

# CULTURED
# COCONUT CREAM

You may be able to find a product online called Coco Jack (coco-jack.com), which allows you to safely and easily remove the tops of coconuts. Otherwise use a meat cleaver or machete with caution.

Reserve your coconut water! It's a delicious and healthy beverage.

 **YOU WiLL NEED...**

3 young coconuts

2 tbsp **coconut water kefir** (p167)

1 litre (1¾ pints) jar

Although often considered a nut, the fruit of the coconut tree is actually a **drupe**, which is a fruit with a layer of outer flesh surrounding a pit of hard endocarp, with a seed inside.

 **METHOD**

**1** Remove the coconut tops and drain the coconut water (this can be reserved for making coconut water kefir, p167).

Coconut water kefir serves as your starter.

**2** With a sturdy metal spoon, remove all flesh from inside the coconut, being careful not to scoop the fibrous husk along with it.

This "rising" during the fermentation process is normal. Simply stir to recombine.

**4** Cover the mouth of the jar with muslin and secure with a rubber band. Leave to sit at room temperature, away from light, for 1 to 2 days. The coconut cream will rise when fermented and develop a tart flavour. When fully fermented, cover with the lid and refrigerate.

**3** In a food processor, combine the coconut flesh and coconut water kefir and blend until very smooth. Transfer to the sterilized jar.

Coconut chutney is perfect with dosa, uttapam, roasted vegetables, or as a savoury spread on bread. Its spicy, tangy flavour can be intensified by adding more chillies.

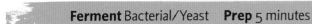

**Ferment** Bacterial/Yeast    **Prep** 5 minutes    **Time** 10 minutes    **Makes** approx 500g (1lb 2oz)

# COCONUT CHUTNEY

Black mustard seeds, dried chiles, urad daal, and asafoetida powder are commonly used in Indian cooking and can be found in Indian grocery stores and spice shops. Here, these spices are tempered, or cooked briefly in hot oil to release their flavour and aroma.

 ## YOU WiLL NEED...

½ tsp salt

2 tsp fresh root ginger, peeled and grated

500g (1lb 2oz) **cultured coconut cream** (pp88–9)

2 tbsp coconut oil

1 tsp black mustard seeds

1 tbsp cumin seeds

2 to 3 whole dried red chillies, such as cayenne

1 tbsp urad daal

A pinch of asafoetida powder

5 to 10 curry leaves, preferably fresh

 ## METHOD

**1** In a medium bowl, mix the salt and fresh ginger into the coconut cream.

**2** To temper the spices, heat the coconut oil in a small pan over medium-high heat. Add the urad daal, mustard seeds, cumin, and chillies.

**3** After 1 to 2 minutes, when the spices start to develop some colour, add the asafoetida powder and curry leaves. Stir for 20 seconds and immediately pour over the coconut cream.

**4** Stir the freshly toasted spices into the coconut cream and serve immediately.

# DAIRY

Cheese, sour cream, yogurt – they're all familiar to most of us, but many people don't realize that they're also fermented foods. In this chapter, you'll learn to make these ferments along with creamy cultured buttermilk, tangy homemade yogurt, and delicious queso fresco.

Cultured butter is smooth, rich, and deeply flavourful, with a slightly tangy, nutty taste that is delicious on toast or when used in cooking. You can also use it to make ghee.

**Ferment** Bacterial     **Prep** 20 minutes     **Time** 6 to 12 hours     **Makes** 450g (1 lb)

# CULTURED BUTTER

When buying cream for butter, look for a variety that has not been pasteurized at ultra high temperature (UHT) and is without additives; these can inhibit fermentation, making it difficult to form butter.

Your jar must be large enough to allow for agitating the cream.

## ⬇ YOU WiLL NEED...

900ml (1½ pints) heavy whipping cream

1 pack buttermilk mesophilic starter (enough for a 1-litre/¾-pint batch)

1 to 2 tsp salt (optional)

2 litre (3½ pint) preserving jar

## ⬇ METHOD

**1** Pour the cream into the sterilized jar and allow it to come to room temperature.

**2** Add the starter to cream and mix thoroughly. Cover the jar tightly with the lid and leave to stand at room temperature for 6 to 12 hours. Longer fermentation will result in a stronger flavour.

**3** Shake the jar vigorously for 10 to 15 minutes. You will see the yellow butter begin to curdle out of the white liquid. Pour off the liquid. This is churned buttermilk, and can be reserved for another use.

To make **ghee**, melt butter in a saucepan over medium heat. Simmer until the top becomes **a deep, translucent yellow.** Decant the yellow butter fat (this is the ghee), leaving the white milk solids behind.

**4** Transfer the butter to a medium bowl. Add cold water to the bowl and rinse the butter, kneading and pressing it to extract excess buttermilk. Discard the cloudy liquid and repeat the rinsing process until the water runs clear. Mix in the salt, if using. Let the butter dry before refrigerating it.

Homemade buttermilk lends a tangy flavour and soft texture to baked goods such as pancakes, scones, and biscuits. It's also a wonderful base for creamy salad dressings.

**Ferment** Bacterial    **Prep** 15 minutes    **Time** 12 to 24 hours    **Makes** 2 litres (3½ pints)

# CULTURED BUTTERMILK

## YOU WILL NEED...

1 litre (1¾ pints) whole milk

2 to 3 tbsp cultured buttermilk (store-bought or homemade) or 1 pack buttermilk mesophilic starter (enough for a 1-litre/¾-pint batch)

1 litre (1¾ pint) preserving jar

## METHOD

1 Pour the milk into the sterilized jar. Add the starter to the milk and stir to mix thoroughly.

2 Cover the mouth of the jar with muslin or kitchen paper and secure with a rubber band.

3 Leave at a warm room temperature (21–26°C /70–78°F) for 12 to 24 hours. At this point, the milk should be thickened and tangy.

4 Cover with the lid and refrigerate. Buttermilk will keep, refrigerated, for 2 to 3 weeks.

The word "buttermilk" can refer to two different products. **Old-fashioned**, or churned, buttermilk is the slightly sour milk left over after churning cream into butter. **Cultured** buttermilk is thicker and creamier, and is made through fermentation.

Kefir is similar to yogurt, but thinner in consistency. It's rich in probiotics and can be consumed on its own, used in smoothies, or strained through muslin overnight to make a creamy cheese.

**Ferment** Bacterial/Yeast     **Prep** 5 minutes     **Time** 12 to 36 hours     **Makes** 2 litres (3½ pints)

# KEFIR

Kefir can be made using kefir grains, but they require daily maintenance. Using a reculturable starter, such as direct-set powdered culture starter, is an easier way to begin. Save a few tablespoons of each batch of kefir to use as a starter for the next.

##  YOU WiLL NEED...

2 litres (3½ pints) milk

1 pack direct-set kefir starter culture (enough for a 2-litre/ 3½ pint batch)

2 litre (3½ pint) preserving jar

##  METHOD

1 Pour the milk into the sterilized jar. Add the starter to the milk and stir to mix thoroughly. Cover tightly with the lid.

2 Leave to sit at room temperature for 12 to 36 hours or until the kefir has reached your preferred level of sourness. Longer fermentation and warmer temperatures will result in a tangier kefir.

3 Transfer to the fridge. Kefir will keep, refrigerated, for several weeks.

The direct-set kefir starter culture can be **purchased from online retailers**. You only need to purchase this for your **first batch**; after that, use **3 tablespoons of reserved kefir** to start each new batch.

Arguably one of the most ubiquitous ferments on earth, yogurt is healthy and delicious. Longer fermentation time reduces lactose content and makes for a tarter yogurt.

**Ferment** Bacterial     **Prep** 90 minutes     **Time** 6 to 24 hours     **Makes** approx 900g (2lb)

# YOGURT

Use store-bought plain yogurt as a starter for your first batch of yogurt, but once you've made your own, you can save a portion of your homemade yogurt and use it to start the next batch.

## YOU WiLL NEED...

2 litres (3½ pints) whole milk

2 tbsp plain yogurt

2 1-litre(1¾-pint) preserving jars

Bottles for hot water

Small cool box

The plain yogurt must have live, active cultures.

## METHOD

Use a thermometer to monitor the temperature. Milk can overheat quickly.

**1** In a stainless steel pan, heat the milk gently to 79°C (175°F), stirring constantly. Remove the pan from the heat and let the milk cool to 43°C (110°F).

**2** Transfer the milk to the sterilized jars, leaving a bit of space for the yogurt starter.

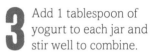

**Heating milk will cause a layer of fat to separate and rise to the top.**

**3** Add 1 tablespoon of yogurt to each jar and stir well to combine.

*You can make yogurt using a reduced fat milk, such as 2% fat, but it will affect the end result. Use* **whole milk** *for a* **rich, creamy yogurt** *that isn't too thin.*

**4** Cover tightly with the lids.

Continued

**5** Warm a small cool box by rinsing the inside with hot water. Place the jars in the cool box, along with a few bottles of hot water (about 52°C/125°F).

Bottles of hot water help maintain a steady, warm environment for the fermenting yogurt.

You can also use a **food dehydrator** with variable temperature control as **an incubation chamber.** Just make sure it stays below 43°C (110°F) to avoid killing the culture.

Wrap the jars well to contain as much of the heat as possible.

**6** Cover the jars and bottles with a scarf or towel and close the cool box. Ferment, undisturbed, for 6 to 24 hours. If fermenting for more than 12 hours, refresh the hot water bottles to maintain an even temperature of 43°C (110°F).

**7** Once it reaches your desired level of tartness, refrigerate the yogurt overnight to allow it to set. Yogurt will keep, refrigerated, for several weeks.

Top the yogurt with dried fruits, chopped nuts, or spices for a high-protein power breakfast.

Homemade yogurt may be a bit **thinner than store-bought yogurt**, which often contains additives for thickening. **Straining** homemade yogurt will create a **thicker texture**.

Tangy Greek yogurt is thick and creamy, rich in protein, and full of beneficial live cultures. Mix with fruit or honey for a satisfying treat, or use as a base for savoury dips and sauces.

**Ferment** Bacterial    **Prep** 5 minutes    **Time** 2 to 5 hours    **Makes** approx 500–675g (1lb 2oz–1½lb)

# GREEK YOGURT

## YOU WILL NEED...

1 litre (1¾ pints) whole milk yogurt

## METHOD

**1** Line a colander with damp muslin or cheesecloth and place it in a large glass bowl.

**2** Pour yogurt into the lined colander and cover it lightly with the muslin. Leave at room temperature for 2 to 3 hours. As the yogurt sits, liquid (whey) will begin to collect in the bowl. Reserve the whey for another use if you like.

**3** After 2 hours, check the consistency of the yogurt. When you are satisfied with the thickness, transfer the yogurt to a sterilized jar and refrigerate. Yogurt will keep, refrigerated, for several weeks.

The whey produced by straining yogurt is rich in **lactic acid bacteria**. Use as a starter for fermented vegetables or in place of water when baking. **Freeze whey** until ready to use.

This is a very easy and rewarding ferment that results in
a sour cream that is richer, thicker, and more flavourful than
those found in the shops. It's also packed with probiotics.

| **Ferment** Bacterial | **Prep time** 40 minutes | **Ferment time** 5+ days | **Makes** approx 900g (2lb) |
| --- | --- | --- | --- |

# SOUR CREAM

##  YOU WiLL NEED...

900g (2lb) double cream

1 pack sour cream mesophilic
   starter (amount adequate for
   1-litre/1¾-pint batch)

1 litre (1¾ pint) jar

##  METHOD

**1** Pour cream into the sterilized jar. Add the starter
to the cream and stir to mix thoroughly. Cover the
mouth of the jar with breathable fabric or kitchen
paper and secure with a rubber band.

**2** Leave at a warm room temperature (21–26°C
/70–78°F) for 1 to 3 days. Check regularly for
sourness and thickness.

**3** When you are satisfied with the results, cover
with the lid and refrigerate. Sour cream will
continue to thicken in the fridge and will keep for
2 to 3 weeks.

In Mexico, sour
cream, or crema, is often
**used to top tacos, taquitos,
tostadas**, and **enchiladas**. In
some Central American
countries, it is served
alongside beans and
fried plantains.

# SIMPLE **CHEESEMAKING** EQUIPMENT

Line the sieve with muslin before using it to strain cheeses.

A **sieve lined with muslin** can be used for straining, or as a simple cheese mould.

Set a **fine mesh sieve** over a **glass bowl** to collect the whey when making fresh cheeses such as queso fresco.

When draining cheeses, **clothes pegs** are an easy and inexpensive option for securing muslin to a colander or bowl.

**S-hooks** are useful for hanging cheeses to drain that have been wrapped in muslin.

If you're new to cheesemaking, you don't need to make a huge investment in equipment. You can accomplish many cheesemaking tasks using everyday items that you may already have at home.

Drain the whey from labneh or other cheeses using a basic **kitchen colander** lined with muslin.

There are over **2,000 varieties of cheese** in the world, and while cheese making may require some time and patience, many simple cheeses can be made right in your kitchen.

A **strawberry basket** lined with muslin can serve as an inexpensive square cheese mould.

**Rubber bands** will keep hanging cheeses tightly wrapped.

**Muslin** is more durable than cheesecloth and can be used to line strainers and moulds, or to hang cheeses to drain.

This tangy cheese is made by straining yogurt until nearly all of the whey has been removed. It is thicker than Greek yogurt, but still soft enough to spread. It's delicious with pitta bread and lends a creamy component to sandwiches.

**Ferment** Bacterial     **Prep** 5 minutes     **Time** 1 to 2 days     **Makes** approx 225g (8oz)

# LABNEH

Labneh is often seasoned with dried herbs and seeds. Try mixing in nigella sativa seeds, dried mint, sumac, or za'atar. You can also roll labneh into balls and coat it with seasonings. To store labneh balls, submerge them in olive oil and refrigerate.

##  YOU WiLL NEED...

1 litre (1¾ pints) whole milk yogurt

## METHOD

1 Line a colander with damp cheesecloth or muslin and place the colander over a clean bowl.

2 Pour the yogurt into the lined colander, cover lightly with muslin or a clean tea towel, and allow the liquid (whey) to drip into the bowl. Leave to sit at room temperature for 12 to 14 hours.

3 When the dripping has slowed to a stop, fold the muslin over the yogurt and put a weight on top to press out the rest of the whey. (A jar of water on a plate works well as a weight.)

4 Check after another 12 hours. Once the cheese is quite dry, transfer it to a jar and refrigerate. Labneh will keep, refrigerated, for several weeks.

In the Middle East, **labneh** is often served as part of a meze, **a selection of appetizers and salads**. Other meze dishes might include hummus, falafel, olives, and flatbread.

This soft goat's cheese is a great introduction to the vast world of cheese making. Its creamy texture and tangy flavour is perfect for spreading on crackers or topping salads.

**Ferment** Bacterial    **Prep** 30 minutes    **Time** 1 to 2 days    **Makes** approx 340g (12oz)

# CHEVRE

Consider coating your fresh chevre with herbs or spices. Some great additions include spearmint, lavender, citrus zest, white sage, and black pepper. To coat the surface, sprinkle herbs on a plate and roll the chevre over them several times until coated.

 **YOU WiLL NEED...**

2 litres (3½ pints) goat's milk

½ pack mesophilic chevre culture (enough for a 2-litre/ 3½-pint batch)

**METHOD**

**1** In a stainless steel pan, heat the milk over a low heat to 29°C (85°F) using a themometer.

Goat's milk is slightly sweeter than cow's milk, and imparts a distinctive earthy flavour to chevre.

**2** Remove from the heat and add the starter, stirring gently. Cover the pan and leave to sit at room temperature for 20 to 24 hours.

**3** Once a strong curd has developed (the curds are visible below the whey), transfer the curds gently to a bowl lined with muslin or cheesecloth.

Save the **leftover whey** from cheesemaking and use it as a **starter for other ferments**, such as Jalepeño hot sauce.

**4** Tie the corners of muslin together and hang over a bowl to collect the whey. Let the cheese hang for 6 hours for a creamy cheese or up to 24 hours for a drier and tangier cheese.

**5** Once it has reached the texture you desire, form into balls or logs, transfer to an airtight container, and refrigerate.

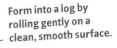

**Form into a log by rolling gently on a clean, smooth surface.**

This fresh Mexican cheese is easy to make and very versatile. Its salty flavour and crumbly texture make it perfect for sprinkling on tacos or salads.

**Ferment** Bacterial    **Prep** 2 hours    **Time** 6 hours    **Makes** 450g (1lb)

# QUESO FRESCO

Queso fresco is traditionally formed into a disk shape, but any style of cheese mould can be used. Try adding chopped jalapeños or dried chillies to the curds in the mould to give it some bite.

##  YOU WiLL NEED...

4 litres (7 pints) milk

1 pack mesophilic starter (enough for a 4-litre/ 7-pint batch)

⅛ tsp rennet diluted in 60ml (2fl oz) water

2 tsp salt

Cheese mould

## METHOD

**1** In a large pan over a medium-high heat, bring the milk to 32°C (90°F) using a thermometer. Remove from the heat, stir in the mesophilic starter and leave to sit, covered, for 40 minutes.

**2** Gently stir in the rennet. Cover and leave to sit for 45 minutes or until the curd is visible below a layer of whey, and pressing into the surface of the curd with a butter knife causes a clean break.

**3** When the cheese has fully set, it will be a semi-solid mass. Cut it with a long knife into 6mm (¼in) cubes. Cover and leave to sit, undisturbed, for 5 minutes.

**4** Return the pan to the stove and slowly heat the curds to 32°C (90°F). Maintaining a constant temperature, stir the curds gently to encourage them to separate from the whey.

**5** With a mesh sieve, strain the curds from the whey, reserving the whey for another use if you like. Place the curds in a cheese mould and mix in the salt.

**6** Cover and set a weight on top of the mould to press the curds into a solid cheese. Leave to sit at room temperature for 4 to 6 hours.

**7** Check after 4 hours. The cheese will become drier the longer it sits in the mould. Refrigerate once you are satisfied with the texture. Cheese will keep, refrigerated, for 1 to 2 weeks.

# LEGUMES AND GRAINS

This chapter draws on culinary traditions from Asia and Central America, and includes the basics of sprouting seeds and grains, how to make tofu from soybeans, how to ferment rice to make Amazake and Tha Bai, and how to make Nixtamal from corn.

This funky ferment is infamous for its pungent aroma and sticky consistency. It's considered a medicinal food and is often served with rice and hot mustard for breakfast.

**Ferment** Bacterial   **Prep** 4 hours   **Ferment** 24 hours   **Makes** approx 900g (2lb)

# NATTO (JAPANESE FERMENTED SOYBEAN)

For your first batch, you'll need to purchase prepared natto from an Asian market. After that, you can save a small amount of homemade natto in the freezer and use it to start your next batch.

 ## YOU WiLL NEED...

200g (7oz) dry soybeans, soaked in water for 6 to 10 hours and then drained

750ml (1¼ pints) water

1 pack plain natto

2 tbsp hot water

2 1-litre (1¾ pints) preserving jars

Bottles for hot water

Small cool box

 ## METHOD

**1** Using a steamer or steamer basket, steam the soybeans for 2 to 4 hours or until they just smash when pinched (cooked, but intact).

**2** In a small bowl, mix 5 to 6 beans from the premade natto with the hot water. Add to the cooked soybeans and mix in thoroughly.

**3** Transfer the inoculated soybeans to the sterilized jars. Cover the mouth of each jar with fabric and secure with a rubber band.

**4** Warm the cool box by rinsing the interior with hot water. Place the jars inside with a few bottles of hot water (about 49°C/120°F).

**5** Cover the jars and water bottles with a scarf or towel and close the box. After 12 hours, refresh the hot water in the jars and ferment for another 12 hours. (Alternatively, incubate in a front-loading food dehydrator at 41°C/105°F for 24 hours.)

**6** The natto is ready when a mouldy film has developed on the soybeans and a stringy texture forms when mixed. Natto will also smell strongly of ammonia.

**7** Cover tightly and refrigerate for 2 to 3 days to allow the ammonia smell to dissipate. Natto will keep, refrigerated, for several weeks. Freeze for longer storage.

In this Japanese ferment, koji transforms starchy rice into a sweet rice pudding. Amazake can be used as a sweetener when baking or eaten on its own as a sugar-free dessert.

**Ferment** Mould   **Prep** 10 minutes   **Time** 8 to 12 hours   **Makes** approx 500g (1lb 2oz)

# AMAZAKE (FERMENTED RICE)

Koji is a mould culture made by inoculating cooked grains or legumes with *Aspergillus oryzae*. It is used in many Japanese fermented foods, including mirin, rice vinegar, and sake. Look for dried koji in Asian markets or purchase through online retailers.

 **YOU WiLL NEED...**

150g (5½oz) short grain white rice (sweet or glutinous variety)

200g (7oz) dried koji

1 litre (1¾ pints) preserving jar

Bottles for hot water

Small cool box

 **METHOD**

**1** Cook the rice according to the package directions.

**2** While rice is still hot, but not above 60°C (140°F), mix the koji in thoroughly. Transfer to the sterilized jar and cover tightly with lid.

**3** Warm the cool box by rinsing the interior with hot water. Place the jar inside along with a few bottles of hot water (about 60°C/140°F).

**4** Cover the jar and water bottles with a scarf or towel and close cooler. Ferment, undisturbed, for 8 to 12 hours. (Alternatively, you can incubate in a front-loading food dehydrator at 52°C/125°F for 8 to 12 hours.)

**5** Check the amazake after 8 hours. It is ready when the rice has developed a porridge-like consistency and a very sweet flavour.

**6** Eat immediately or, for long storage, boil the amazake to stop fermentation and refrigerate. Amazake will keep, refrigerated, for 1 to 2 weeks.

The crisp and savoury dosa is a South Indian flatbread made without wheat or gluten. It is a nutritious alternative to tortillas, pancakes, and pittas and can be used for wraps or dipping.

**Ferment** Lacto    **Prep** 1 hour    **Time** 2 to 3 days    **Makes** 30 dosa

# DOSA

Dosa are best eaten immediately, but the batter can be made up to a week ahead and kept in the refrigerator until ready for use. Just thin with water as needed before using.

### YOU WiLL NEED...

400g (14oz) rice (any variety)

200g (7oz) lentils (any variety)

1 tbsp fenugreek seeds

50g (1¾oz) chana daal (optional)

2 tsp salt

4 tbsp ghee, butter, or oil

Lentils come in **several varieties** including brown, yellow, black, red, and green. **Any variety** may be used for dosa, however, green lentils are harder and may be more difficult to blend.

### METHOD

**1** In two separate bowls, soak the rice and lentils in spring or filtered water for 8 to 10 hours. Soak the fenugreek and chana daal (if using) with the lentils.

Add enough water to fully cover rice and lentils.

**2** Drain the rice and discard the soaking water. Transfer the rice to a blender and mix into a thin batter, adding soaking water from lentils as necessary. Pour the batter into a 4-litre (7-pint) jar or stainless steel pan.

The lentil batter should have a thick but pourable consistency.

**3** Transfer the lentils, fenugreek, and chana daal to the blender, along with the remainder of their soaking water. Blend to a thin batter, adding more spring or filtered water if necessary. Combine with the blended rice in the jar. Add the salt and mix the batter to fully incorporate the rice and lentils.

**4** Cover the mouth of the jar with fabric and a rubber band so the ferment can breathe. Leave to sit at room temperature (at least 21°C/70°F) for 1 to 2 days or until it has risen significantly.

Continued

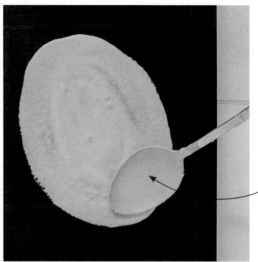

**Spread the batter thinly for a crisp, crepe-like texture.**

**6** To cook, heat a cast iron pan or griddle over a medium heat until it barely begins to smoke. Sprinkle with a small amount of water and wipe it clean. With a large spoon, add about 4 tablespoons of batter to the cooking surface and quickly spread it in a circular motion, evening out any thick spots as you go.

**5** Stir the batter and, if necessary, add more water. The batter should be a bit thinner than pancake batter but thick enough to coat the back of a spoon.

**Softening the butter will make it easier to spread on the surface of the dosa.**

To make **masala dosa**, spread a thin layer of tomato sauce over the surface of the dosa after adding the ghee and top with raw onions and peppers, potato masala, and garam masala.

**7** Add ½ teaspoon of ghee, butter, or oil to the surface of the dosa. Let it cook until the dosa begins to brown and the edges curl up, about 2 minutes. It should easily release from the pan. Flipping it is optional, but not necessary.

**8** Serve immediately with the toppings and accompaniments of your choice.

A **common street food** in South India, dosa are often served with **chutney and sambar,** a hearty lentil and vegetable stew

Uttapam is similar to dosa, but it is thick and soft rather than thin and crepe-like. Vegetables and spices are cooked into the batter, creating a satisfying stuffed pancake.

**Ferment** Bacterial    **Prep** 1 hour    **Time** 2 to 3 days    **Makes** 25 uttapam

# UTTAPAM

Uttapam is spiced with fenugreek, chana daal, and garam masala, which can be found in Indian shops or speciality stores. Any finely chopped vegetables can be added to the uttapam while cooking. Try adding chillies for heat and serving with fruit chutney.

## YOU WILL NEED...

400g (14oz) basmati rice

200g (7oz) dry lentils (any variety)

1 tbsp fenugreek seeds

50g (1¾oz) chana daal (optional)

2 tsp salt

2 tbsp ghee, butter, or olive oil

2 tomatoes, thinly sliced

1 red onion, thinly sliced

2 green chillies or bell peppers, thinly sliced

1 tbsp garam masala powder

## METHOD

1 Place the rice in a medium bowl and add filtered water to cover. Place the lentils, fenugreek, and chana daal (if using) in a second bowl and add filtered water to cover. Soak both overnight.

2 Drain the rice and discard the soaking water. In a blender or food processor, combine the soaked rice, lentils, fenugreek, and chana daal (if using), along with the soaking liquid from the lentils. Blend until smooth.

3 Transfer the batter to a large bowl. Add salt and mix thoroughly. Cover with a clean cloth or tea towel.

4 Set aside to ferment at room temperature for 12 to 48 hours, or until the batter has risen significantly and taken on a slightly sour smell.

5 Heat a cast iron pan over a medium heat. Add about 4 tablespoons of batter to the pan and quickly spread in a circle. Drizzle ¼ teaspoon of ghee over the batter surface and sprinkle with some of the onion, bell pepper, tomato, and a small pinch of garam masala.

6 After 4 to 5 minutes, or once the underside is golden brown, flip and cook on the other side until cooked through. Repeat with the remaining batter and vegetables.

# SOAKING & SPROUTING
## SEEDS, BEANS, & GRAINS

A good home-sprouting setup is inexpensive and easy to prepare. It can be used for sprouting seeds, grains, or beans, but there are some important things to know when putting together your sprouting environment.

### USE THE RIGHT CONTAINERS

Kilner jars with plastic rings and mesh screens are used to make sprouting vessels that drain. Wire mesh sprouting screens of varying sizes can be purchased online, or you can make your own. Smaller grains and seeds will require a finer mesh, while a more open mesh can be used for larger grains and nuts. Always use the widest mesh possible for optimal drainage.

**Sprouting vessels**
Simple kilner jars will suffice, but be sure to use plastic lid rings during soaking and sprouting, as metal rings can rust over time.

Use fresh, clean water for rinsing and soaking.

Use the largest screen size possible for optimum drainage and airflow.

### KNOW THE SOAKING AND SPROUTING TIMES

Different types of grains, seeds, and legumes require different soaking and sprouting times. The following sprouting chart includes the soak and sprout times for some common varieties. The amount will vary based on the type of grain, seed, or bean you use.

| SPROUT | SOAK TIME | SPROUT TIME |
| --- | --- | --- |
| Beans (any variety) | 10–12 hours | 3–5 days |
| Chickpeas | 12 hours | 2–4 days |
| Lentils | 6–8 hours | 3-4 days |
| Quinoa | 3–4 hours | 2-3 days |
| Spelt | 6 hours | 1–2 days |
| Teff | 3–4 hours | 1–2 days |
| Peas | 8 hours | 2–3 days |
| Pumpkin seeds | 6 hours | 1–2 days |
| Alfalfa | 12 hours | 3–5 days |
| Mustard seeds | 5 hours | 3–5 days |
| Radish seeds | 6 hours | 3  5 days |
| Rye | 6–8 hours | 2–3 days |
| Wheat | 8–10 hours | 2–3 days |
| Millet | 5 hours | 12 hours |
| Soybean | 4–8 hours | 3–4 days |

# KEEP THESE TIPS IN MIND

• Prior to sprouting, store dry seeds, grains, and beans in sealed jars or bags.
• When rinsing your seeds, use fresh, cold water.
• Seeds and grains can be soaked overnight directly in the vessel in which they'll be sprouting.
• Afer soaking, move your sprouting container to an area with plenty of light to facilitate the sprouting process.

• Keep the sprouting jar tilted down so that water pools toward the the mouth of the jar. This will keep the sprouts moist, but not soaked.
• Make sure there is plenty of air circulation and that sprouts are drained properly. Too much moisture will encourage mould growth.
• Store sprouted seeds in a closed container in the refrigerator to keep them fresh and dry.

**Eating sprouts**
Sprouts are incredibly healthy and can be eaten on their own, sprinkled on salads, or dried and ground into sprouted flour.

You can replace the mesh insert with a breathable fabric after sprouting.

Sprouted grains are vitamin-rich and easily digestible. Soaking neutralizes phytic acid, a compound that prevents the body from fully absorbing nutrients. Enjoy sprouted grains either raw or dehydrated and ground into flour.

**Ferment** Non-fermenting    **Prep** 5 minutes    **Time** 1 to 5 days    **Makes** approx 50–70g (1¾ to 2½oz)

# SPROUTED GRAIN

##  YOU WILL NEED...

4 tbsp whole, dry grain, such as wheat berries, rice, or quinoa

350ml (12fl oz) water, plus more for rinsing

1 litre (1¾ pints) jar with mesh lid

##  METHOD

**1** Add the grain to the jar and pour in the water. Cover the jar with a mesh sprouting lid and allow the grain to soak for 6 to 12 hours, depending on how hearty the grain is.

**2** Strain the water from the grain, rinse, and place at a slight angle with the mouth of the jar angled down to allow the grains to drain fully.

**3** Rinse and drain 2 to 4 times a day until you see the germ begin to pop out at the tip of the grain. The grains are now sprouted and ready to be eaten, or dehydrate and use to make sprouted flour.

Many grains are suitable for sprouting, but some may take **longer to sprout** or require **more frequent rinsing**. Consult a **sprouting chart** for specific sprouting and rinsing guidelines.

Rejuvelac is a fresh, tangy tonic beverage made with sprouted grain. It contains beneficial bacteria and enzymes that can aid in digestion, and can be used in place of water when baking bread.

**Ferment** Bacterial     **Prep** 5 minutes     **Time** 1 to 2 days     **Makes** approx 1 litre (1¾ pints)

# REJUVELAC

 ## YOU WILL NEED...

65–100g (2–3½oz) freshly sprouted
   grain, such as brown rice
   or quinoa

1 litre (1¾ pints) water

1 litre (1¾ pints) jar

 ## METHOD

1 Place the grains in the jar (or leave them in the jar in which they were sprouted).

2 Add enough water to the jar to submerge the grains, leaving about 2.5cm (1in) of headspace.

3 Place a piece of breathable fabric, such as muslin, over the mouth of the jar and secure with a rubber band. Leave to sit at room temperature, away from light, for 1 to 2 days.

4 Rejuvelac is ready when the water has developed a light, cloudy appearance and fresh, lemony taste. Strain the rejuvelac from the grains and refrigerate. It will keep, refrigerated, for 1 to 2 weeks.

The grains leftover from making rejuvelac are **very fermented and easy to digest**. They share the tart, lemony flavour of rejuvelac. Mix them into bread dough or use them to coat the surface of a loaf for an added **boost of nutrition** and flavour.

This versatile protein source is an integral part of East Asian and Southeast Asian cuisines. Freshly made, it is warm and creamy, with a firm but yielding texture.

**Ferment** Non-fermenting    **Prep** 12 hours    **Time** 20 to 50 minutes    **Makes** 450g (1lb)

# TOFU

Tofu is made by adding a solidifying agent, such as nigari, to hot soy milk. Nigari (magnesium chloride derived from sea water), causes the proteins and oils in soy milk to coagulate, creating curds that can be pressed into tofu. Nigari can be found in Japanese stores and online.

 **YOU WiLL NEED...**

400g (14oz) dry soybeans

1.5 litres (2¾ pints) plus 4 litres (7 pints) water

4 tbsp nigari (magnesium chloride)

 **METHOD**

**1** In a medium bowl, combine 1.5 litres (2¾ pints) of the water and soybeans. Set aside to soak for 8 to 12 hours, or overnight.

**2** In a blender, combine the soybeans and soaking water and blend for 4 to 5 minutes, or until smooth and uniformly white.

**3** In a very large pan, combine the blended soybeans and the 4 litres (7 pints) of water. Bring to a boil over a high heat, then simmer for 15 to 20 minutes, stirring frequently to prevent boiling over.

**4** Strain the contents of the pan through a muslin-lined colander, reserving the liquid. The liquid is soy milk and the solid pulp is called okara. Return the soymilk to the pan. (The okara can be discarded or used for baking or vegetable patties.)

**5** Heat the soy milk to 82°C (180°F). Add the nigari, stir gently, and wait 5 to 10 minutes for the soymilk to curdle and the liquid portion to become clear. If the liquid isn't clear after 10 minutes, add an additional tablespoon of nigari, stir gently, and wait for 5 more minutes.

**6** Once curds have formed and the liquid is clear, transfer the contents of the pan to a clean, muslin-lined strainer.

**7** Fold over or tie the muslin and place a jar of water on top to press the liquid out of the tofu. For soft tofu, remove from the strainer after 20 minutes. For extra-firm tofu, remove after 50 minutes.

**8** Transfer the tofu to an airtight container and add fresh water until it is submerged. Cover and refrigerate. Use the tofu within 1 to 2 weeks.

For a complete **change of texture**, try turning your firm tofu into **spongy tofu**. Simply freeze the tofu overnight, thaw the next day, and press to remove all water. Spongy tofu is great for grilling or stir-trying.

This Cambodian fermented rice dessert is chewy and alcoholic, with a flavour reminiscent of sweet saki. Serve on its own or topped with shredded coconut.

**Ferment** Bacterial/Mould/Yeast    **Prep** 5 minutes    **Time** 2 to 3 days    **Makes** approx 800g (1¾lb)

# THA BAI (CAMBODIAN FERMENTED RICE)

Fermenting for longer than 3 days will yield a more strongly alcoholic dessert. If you prefer it sweet, you can either eat it while still young or add sweetener to balance the alcohol level.

##  YOU WiLL NEED...

400g (14oz) black rice

1 litre (1¾ pints) water

2 jiuqu (Shanghai yeast balls)

2 tbsp honey, maple syrup, or molasses (optional)

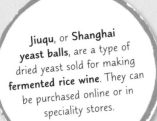

Jiuqu, or **Shanghai yeast balls**, are a type of dried yeast sold for making **fermented rice wine**. They can be purchased online or in speciality stores.

## METHOD

**1** In a mesh strainer, rinse the rice two or three times. Place the rice and water in a pan and cover. Cook over a low heat until all the water is absorbed.

**2** Once the rice is cooked, turn off the heat and cool to room temperature.

**3** With a pestle and mortar, crush the yeast balls and grind to a fine powder.

**4** Spread the rice in a medium Pyrex or ceramic dish with a lid. Using a sieve, sprinkle the yeast ball powder evenly over the surface of the rice. Mix thoroughly and cover with the lid.

**5** Wrap the covered dish with a towel, blanket, or scarf and place in a warm, dark place to incubate and ferment for 2 to 3 days.

**6** Sweeten with honey, maple syrup, or molasses (if needed) and refrigerate. Tha bai will keep, refrigerated, for 2 to 3 weeks, but may become more strongly alcoholic over time.

Nixtamal, or hominy, is made by soaking corn kernels in pickling lime, which increases their nutritional value and makes them easier to digest. Grind nixtamal to make your own fresh masa, or corn dough.

**Ferment** Non-fermenting    **Prep** 90 minutes    **Time** 12 hours    **Makes** 800g (1¾lb)

# NIXTAMAL

Nixtamal starts with dent corn, or field corn, which is very different from the familiar sweet corn found in the supermarket. It can be purchased online or from some natural food stores.

## ⬇ YOU WILL NEED...

1.5 litres (2¾ pints) water

2 tbsp pickling lime (also known as calcium hydroxide)

400g (14oz) dry dent corn kernels, rinsed

Dent corn kernels are large and have a thick skin that must be removed before eating.

## ⬇ METHOD

**1** In a stainless steel pan, combine the water and pickling lime. (Take care when using pickling lime; it is caustic and can irritate the skin. Rinse with water if it comes in contact with skin.)

**2** Add the corn kernels to the pot and bring the contents to a boil. Lower the heat and simmer for 1 hour. Remove from the heat, cover, and leave for 8 to 10 hours at room temperature.

**3** Pour off the liquid and rinse the corn, agitating to loosen and remove all the skins. Rinse 4 to 6 times or until water runs clear.

**The skins should come off easily and can be discarded.**

Whole kernels are perfect for use in soups.

**4** The nixtamal can now be used whole or ground into dough using a food processor. Use within 1 to 2 days or freeze for future use.

# BREAD

After tasting the rich, complex flavours of fermented breads, you'll never want a store-bought loaf again. In this chapter, you'll learn how to begin a sourdough starter and make your own crusty sourdough bread; how to make tangy injera, an Ethiopian flat bread; and how to make nutty buckwheat buttermilk pancakes.

Gorditas are thick Mexican corn cakes made with masa. Freshly baked, these soft and chewy "little fat ones" can be split and filled with your choice of meats, cheeses, or vegetables.

**Ferment** Non-fermenting　　**Prep** 20 minutes　　**Time** 25 minutes　　**Makes** 6 gorditas

# GORDITAS

Fresh masa can be purchased at speciality shops, or you can make nixtamal and grind your own masa from scratch. Masa should be finely ground for a smooth dough.

## YOU WiLL NEED...

1 tsp baking powder

¼ tsp salt

200g (7oz) fresh, smooth-ground corn masa (nixtamalized corn dough)

4 tbsp water

## METHOD

**1** Preheat the oven to 230°C (450°F).

**2** In a medium bowl, add the baking powder and salt to the masa and mix to combine.

**3** Roll 2 tablespoons of dough into a ball to test its consistency. It should be dry enough to hold its shape, but moist enough that it doesn't crack when the ball is formed. Add water in small amounts until you reach the desired consistency.

**4** Form the dough into 6 equally sized balls (about 2 tbsp each). With the palms of your hands, flatten each ball into a disk of even thickness and place on a lightly oiled baking sheet.

**5** Bake for 25 minutes or until the gorditas are golden and cooked through. Gorditas are best enjoyed fresh, so only cook as many as you plan to eat and save the rest for later.

This Ethiopian flatbread is sour and spongy with a great chewiness. Its flavour and texture pair perfectly with traditional Ethiopian meat and vegetable dishes.

**Ferment** Bacterial/Yeast    **Prep** 5 minutes    **Time** 2 to 3 days    **Makes** 2 to 3 injera

# INJERA

Injera is often served piled with a variety of braised meat, vegetable, and legume dishes called *wots*. Pieces of the pliable flatbread are torn off and used to scoop up the savoury wots by hand.

 ## YOU WiLL NEED...

225g (8oz) teff flour (available in speciality stores and online)

500ml (16fl oz) water

½ tsp baking powder

¼ tsp salt

1 litre (1¾ pint) jar

 ## METHOD

**1** In the sterilized jar, combine the teff flour and water and mix well. Cover the mouth of jar with fabric and secure with a rubber band.

**2** Leave to sit at room temperature for 2 to 3 days, stirring at least twice a day to aerate the batter and encourage yeast activity.

**3** Once the batter has begun to bubble visibly, stir in the baking powder and salt and leave to stand for at least 20 minutes.

**4** Preheat a 25cm (10in) cast iron griddle or pan over a medium-high heat. Add a few drops of oil to the pan. Pour 120ml (4fl oz) of batter into the pan and tilt to coat the surface with batter.

**5** When bubbles appear over the entire surface of the batter, cover with a lid to allow the steam to build up and cook the surface, about 3 to 5 minutes.

**6** Remove from the pan and place between two napkins to keep warm while you cook the remaining injera.

These gluten-free pancakes have a nutty, slightly sour flavour and a tender texture. They are delicious with cultured coconut cream, fruit, and maple syrup.

**Ferment** Bacterial     **Prep** 15 minutes     **Time** 20 minutes     **Makes** 8 pancakes

# BUCKWHEAT BUTTERMILK PANCAKES

If you can't get hold of buttermilk, substitute 225g (8oz) plain yogurt (not Greek) and 120ml (4fl oz) of water. You can also replace half of the buckwheat flour with teff flour, which makes for a balanced complement to the buckwheat.

##  YOU WILL NEED...

350ml (12fl oz) **cultured buttermilk** (p96)

1 egg

1 tbsp coconut oil or butter

150g (5½oz) buckwheat flour

⅔ tsp baking powder

¼ tsp baking soda

¼ tsp salt

## METHOD

1 In a medium bowl, whisk together the buttermilk, egg, and coconut oil.

2 In another bowl, mix the buckwheat flour, baking powder, baking soda, and salt.

3 Add the dry ingredients to the wet ingredients and stir until fully incorporated.

4 Let the batter rest for at least 20 minutes at room temperature or overnight in the fridge.

5 Heat a cast iron skillet over a low heat. Grease the pan with a small amount of coconut oil or butter.

6 Pour batter in small portions onto the skillet and cook until bubbles form on the surface. Flip and cook for another 30 seconds or so, until just cooked through. Keep warm until serving.

# MAKING & USING
## SOURDOUGH STARTERS

Sourdough starters are living, active cultures that contain wild yeasts and lactic acid bacteria. Before commercial baker's yeast became available, sourdough starters were the primary method for keeping active yeast ready for baking.

Sourdough starters require a little bit of care and maintenance, but once you have one, chewy, delicious sourdough is never far away. Due to the action of the wild microorganisms on the wheat, naturally leavened breads made with sourdough starter have a different flavour profile and greater nutritional value than commercially yeasted bread. The character of the sourdough starter will affect the flavour of the finished bread. Try using your starter for sourdough bread, purple amazake sourdough, or sourdough pizza. Sourdough starter can also be used to start wild beverage ferments.

### MAKING A SOURDOUGH STARTER

**1** In a 2-litre (3½-pint) sterilized jar, combine 300g (10oz) of flour (whole wheat or all-purpose) and 480ml (15½fl oz) of water.

**2** Stir to mix thoroughly.

**3** Cover the mouth of the jar with breathable fabric and secure with a rubber band. Set in a warm place to ferment.

**5** Once the starter begins bubbling, it is ready to be primed for use in baking. To prime, add 40g (1½oz) of flour and 2 tbsp of water every 8 hours for 24 hours, mixing well after each addition.

## USING YOUR STARTER

Store your starter in a closed jar in the fridge and feed it on the day before you use it, after use, and at least once every 2 to 3 days. If the starter becomes too big for the jar, discard a portion. With proper care, your starter will last indefinitely.

## SAVING A NEGLECTED STARTER

Sourdough starters are nearly indestructible, but if you neglect one for too long, it can become alcoholic and/or mouldy. To revive, pour the liquid off the surface and feed twice a day, stirring well, until it begins to bubble vigorously and smell fruity.

## SOURDOUGH TO SHARE

To share a sourdough starter, give 40g (1½oz) of your sourdough starter to a friend. If they add 480ml (15½fl oz) of water and 300g (10oz) flour, stir, cover the mouth of the jar with fabric. Their starter will develop quickly and should be ready for use within 2 to 4 days.

**4** Feed the starter once a day until it begins to bubble (usually about 7–10 days) each day add 40g (1½oz) of flour and 2 tbsp of water and stir well.

This chewy loaf has tart overtones and a unique expression of wheat flavour. The crunchy crust contrasts beautifully with the fluffy inner crumb. Enjoy plain, with cultured butter, dipped in quality olive oil, or as part of a sauerkraut sandwich.

**Ferment** Bacterial/Yeast    **Prep** 3 hours    **Time** 12 to 24 hours    **Makes** 1 loaf

# SOURDOUGH BREAD

Making a sourdough loaf requires time and patience, so don't rush the process – a really good loaf is worth the wait. For added depth of flavour, add seeds or whole spices to the surface of your loaf for an impressive presentation and wonderful taste.

## YOU WiLL NEED...

300ml (10fl oz) water

100g (3½oz) sourdough starter

425g (15oz) all-purpose flour

1 tsp salt

2 tbsp whole seeds and spices (optional)

Pizza stone or other baking surface

## METHOD

1 In a large mixing bowl, combine the water and sourdough starter.

Sourdough generally calls for all-purpose (white) flour, however, you can **vary the flavour** by using other flours such as **rye flour** or **whole-grain wheat flour.**

For the best flavour, use filtered water.

**2** Add the flour, mix until the water is fully absorbed and a shaggy dough forms. Cover with a towel and rest for 20 minutes.

**4** Cover with a damp tea towel and leave for 1½ hours. Every 30 minutes, fold the dough in on itself from all four corners. Keep the dough covered between foldings.

Every sourdough culture is a bit different and the **time to proof** (rise) can vary based on the **characteristics of the starter.** Try adjusting the proofing to improve your loaf.

Add some tension as you pull and fold the dough in on itself.

**3** Sprinkle salt evenly on surface and knead dough for 5 to 10 minutes or until a completely consistent dough is achieved.

Continued

**5** Cover the dough with a damp tea towel and leave, undisturbed, for 6 to 8 hours or until it has doubled in size.

**6** Fold and shape the dough into a ball, cover and leave to rest for 20 minutes. (At this point, if using seeds or spices, spread them on a clean surface and roll the dough over them to coat it.)

Try adding seeds or whole spices to the surface of your loaf. **Sesame seeds, sunflower seeds, cumin, or caraway** are all good options. Mix and match to suit your tastes.

**Keep the board well floured so the dough doesn't stick.**

**7** Shape again, tightly this time, and transfer, upside down, to a bowl coated with olive oil. Cover and allow to rest for 1½ to 2 hours at room temperature.

**8** Preheat the oven and baking surface to 240°C (475°F/Gas 9). Transfer the dough directly onto the hot baking surface, score the top with a bread knife, and bake for 10 minutes. Lower the heat to 200°C (400°F/Gas 6) and bake for another 25 minutes. Remove from the oven and transfer to a cutting board or cooling rack. Allow to rest for 15 to 30 minutes before slicing.

The maintenance of your starter will affect the final flavour of your bread. For a **less sour flavour,** pour off the top half of the starter before feeding.

This pizza crust recipe makes enough dough for six small pizzas, so you can customize the toppings to suit every taste. Try the classic flavours of tomato, basil, and mozzarella.

**Ferment** Bacterial / Yeast    **Prep** 3 hours    **Time** 8 hours    **Makes** 6 pizzas

# SOURDOUGH PIZZA

If you want to prepare the dough well in advance, follow steps 1 to 6 and then freeze it. Allow at least 2 hours for it to thaw and come to room temperature before stretching. Brushing the surface with olive oil will give it a nice shine and crisp texture.

 ## YOU WiLL NEED...

480ml (16fl oz) water

200g (7oz) sourdough starter

850g (1¾lb) flour

2 tsp salt

Sauce and toppings of
  your choice

 ## METHOD

**1** In a large mixing bowl, combine the water and sourdough starter. Add the flour and mix until the water is fully absorbed and a shaggy dough forms. Cover with a damp tea towel and leave to rest for 20 minutes.

**2** Sprinkle salt evenly over the surface and knead the dough for 5 to 10 minutes or until a completely consistent texture is achieved.

**3** Cover with a damp tea towel and leave for 1½ hours. Every 30 minutes, fold the dough in on itself from all four corners. Keep the dough covered between foldings.

**4** After the last folding, leave the dough covered and leave it to sit, undisturbed, for 6 to 8 hours.

**5** Divide the dough into 6 pieces. Fold and shape each piece into a ball and coat with flour. Place on a baking sheet and cover with a damp tea towel. Leave at room temperature for 1½ to 2 hours or until the balls have doubled in size.

**6** Place a pizza stone or other baking surface in the oven and preheat oven to 240°C (475°F/Gas 9).

**7** On a well-floured cutting board, stretch and spread each ball of dough to your desired size and thickness. The thinner you make your dough, the crispier it will be. Add the sauce and toppings of your choice.

**8** Slide the pizzas from the cutting board onto the preheated baking surface and bake for 12 to 15 minutes or until the crusts are lightly browned.

This sourdough recipe calls for amazake, a fermented rice porridge made with sticky black rice. It lends a light sweetness to the bread as well as a strikingly beautiful purple colour.

**Ferment** Bacterial/Yeast/Mould     **Prep** 12 to 24 hours     **Time** 35 minutes     **Makes** 1 loaf

# PURPLE AMAZAKE
## SOURDOUGH

 ### YOU WiLL NEED...

276g (10oz) water

100g (3½oz) sourdough starter

475g (1lb 1oz) flour

1½ tsp salt

200g (7oz) sticky black rice **amazake** (p118), boiled, cooled, and strained

1 tsp olive oil

 ### METHOD

**1** In a large mixing bowl, mix the water and sourdough starter. Reserve 2 tablespoons of flour and add the rest to the bowl. Mix until a shaggy dough forms. Cover with a damp tea towel and leave for 20 minutes.

**2** Sprinkle 1 teaspoon of salt evenly over the surface and knead the dough for 5 to 10 minutes or until a consistent texture is achieved.

**3** In a small bowl, mix the amazake, the remaining ½ teaspoon of salt, and remaining 2 tablespoons of flour. Add the amazake and flour mixture to the dough, folding and kneading to combine.

**4** Cover and leave for 1½ hours. Every 30 minutes, fold the dough in on itself from all four corners. Keep it covered between foldings.

**5** Cover and leave to sit for 6 to 8 hours or until it has doubled in size. Fold and shape the dough into a ball, adding enough flour as needed to keep it from sticking to your hands. Cover and rest for 20 minutes.

**6** Lightly coat a large bowl with olive oil. Shape the dough again and place in the bowl, seam side down. Cover for 1½ to 2 hours.

**7** Place a baking surface (cast iron, baking stone, or ceramic baking pan) in the oven and preheat the oven to 240°C (475°F/Gas 9).

**8** Transfer the dough directly onto the preheated baking surface, score the top with a razor blade or bread knife, and bake for 10 minutes. Reduce the heat to 220°C (425°F/Gas 7) and bake for 25 minutes more.

**9** Remove from oven and transfer to a cutting board or cooling rack. Rest for 15 to 30 minutes before slicing.

# BEVERAGES

One of the beautiful things about fermentation is the pure simplicity of the process –take a few basic ingredients, process them under the right conditions, and watch them transform into something new. Nowhere is this more evident than with the beverage ferments you'll find in this chapter.

A ginger bug is a cultivated wild yeast culture that can be used to start ferments. Use this in any beverage that needs yeast to carbonate or become alcoholic.

**Ferment** Wild Yeast     **Prep** 15 minutes     **Time** 5 to 7 days     **Makes** approx 100g (3½oz)

# GINGER BUG

 ## YOU WiLL NEED...

50g (1¾oz) fresh root ginger, grated with skin on

100g (3½oz) sugar

240ml (8fl oz) water

Ginger bug can be used as a **starter for any alcoholic beverage.** To use, strain a few tablespoons of liquid from the jar and add it to your fermentation vessel.

 ## METHOD

**1** In a small sterilized jar, combine 1 tablespoon of grated ginger, 1 tablespoon of sugar, and the water. Mix together well.

**2** Cover the mouth of the jar with a breathable fabric, such as muslin, and secure with a rubber band.

**3** Leave to sit at room temperature for 4 to 6 days. Every day, add 1 tablespoon of grated ginger and 1 tablespoon of sugar to the jar, mix well, and cover again.

**4** Once the ginger bug has a yeasty smell and is actively bubbling, it is ready for use. Store in the fridge and occasionally release the pressure in the jar. Ginger bug will keep for several months.

Herbal syrups impart flavour and medicinal benefits to fermented beverages. Any culinary or medicinal herb can be used to make herbal syrup. Experiment with combinations of fresh herbs, whole spices, and aromatics.

**Ferment** Boil    **Prep** 5 minutes    **Time** 30 minutes    **Makes** approx 450ml (15fl oz)

# HERBAL SYRUP

 ## YOU WiLL NEED...

720ml (1¼ pints) water

50g (1¾oz) whole spices or aromatics of your choice

5 to 8 sprigs fresh herbs of your choice

700g (1½lb) honey or sugar

 ## METHOD

**1** In a saucepan over a medium-high heat, combine the water and any "sturdy" aromatics you choose to use, such as ginger root or cinnamon. Boil for 15 minutes. (If you are using leafy herbs only, simply bring the water to a boil.)

**2** Remove from the heat and add more delicate herbal additions, such as fresh leaves and flowers. Steep for 15 minutes.

**3** With a fine mesh sieve, strain the liquid into a sterilized jar or glass jug, squeezing to extract all liquid from the plant matter. Add the honey or sugar and stir to dissolve.

**4** Transfer the syrup to a sterilized swing stopper bottle or a jar with a tight-fitting lid using a sterilized funnel. Herbal syrups will keep, refrigerated, for up to 2 months.

**Fresh herbs** to try include peppermint, rosemary, thyme, and basil. Add **spice** with ginger, cinnamon sticks, whole cloves, or cardamom. **Other additions** include citrus rind and orange blossoms.

# BOTTLING & CARBONATING

Bottling and carbonating beverages is a simple process, and seeing your beverages transformed into bubbly, fizzy concoctions is well worth the effort.

## BOTTLING

For small batches, bottles can be easily filled using a clean funnel. For batches of more than 11 litres (3 gallons) in volume, a siphon is more practical and can be made even more convenient with the use of a spring-loaded bottle filler.

When bottling for carbonation, use strong, thick bottles that can seal tightly, such as swing stopper bottles, crown cap, or champagne-style bottles. The last two require special presses to cap or cork the bottles, while swing stopper bottles can be used and reused with no extra equipment.

## CARBONATING

Once your fermented beverage is bottled, keep the bottles at room temperature for anywhere from 1 day to 2 weeks. To check the level of carbonation, unscrew the cap slightly or release the swing top momentarily and listen for the release of gas. If you hear gas escaping, it should be carbonated enough to refrigerate and enjoy. If not, quickly reseal it and give it more time. Every time you open a bottle, $CO_2$ is released and the pressurization has to start from scratch. For this reason, it is best to check only one bottle from each batch and to do this no more than once a day.

## FACTORS THAT AFFECT CARBONATION

• The amount of sugar in the liquid when you bottle it directly affects the amount of carbonation that will build up. More sugar means more carbonation, which is why extra sugar is sometimes added before bottling. This is called *priming*.

• The type of sugar used can also affect carbonation. Yeast consumes some sugars more easily than others. For example, the sugars in pineapple, grape, and peach juices break down very quickly, while the sugars in blueberries and strawberries are slower to ferment.

• Ambient temperature has a significant impact on speed of carbonation. Yeast acts more slowly in the cold and will become dormant at temperatures below 4°C (40°F). On a hot summer day, carbonation may happen much more quickly than you'd expect, while in the winter months it can take a while longer.

• The amount of headspace in the bottle can help or prohibit carbonation. If the bottle is only half full, more fermentation is needed to pressurize and carbonate the liquid. When filling 750ml (1¼ pint) bottles, leave 5–7.5cm (2–3in) of headspace in the neck. For 350ml (12oz) bottles, leave about 5cm (2in) of headspace.

## YEAST CONSUMES SUGARS

▷

## CREATING CO2 WHICH BUILDS UP AND IS TRAPPED IN THE BOTTLE

▷

## FORCING IT TO DISSOLVE INTO THE LIQUID

If you've opened a shaken can of fizzy drink, you know how **messy over-carbonated** beverages can be. Always open bottles **outside** or **over the sink** and have an empty glass ready to catch the **overflow** of foam.

When too much **pressure** builds up, carbonating beverages can **explode**. To avoid messy disasters, keep carbonating bottles in a **milk crate** lined with two bin bags. If a bottle does explode, they will contain most of the mess.

This refreshing, non-alcoholic summer beverage can be enjoyed by kids and adults alike. The fermented ginger and citrus cleanse the palate and aid in digestion.

**Ferment** Yeast     **Prep** 45 minutes     **Time** 3 to 4 days     **Makes** 1 litre (1¾ pints)

# GINGER BEER

## YOU WiLL NEED...

2.5–7.5cm (1–3in) piece fresh root ginger, grated or sliced

2 litres (3½ pints) water

100g (3½oz) sugar

Juice of 1 small lemon or 2 limes

3 tbsp **ginger bug** (p156), strained

2 litre (3½ pints) jar

Bottles for bottling

## METHOD

**1** In a small pan, combine the ginger and 1 litre (1¾ pints) water. Bring to a boil over a high heat and boil for 15 minutes.

**2** Place a mesh sieve over the jar and strain the ginger infusion into it. Do not discard the ginger.

**3** Return the ginger to the pan and add the remaining water. Bring to a boil over a high heat and boil for 15 minutes.

**4** Strain the second batch of ginger infusion into the jar. The ginger can either be saved for another use or discarded.

**5** Add the sugar to the jar and stir to dissolve. Allow the liquid to cool to room temperature.

**6** Add the lemon or lime juice and ginger bug to the jar. Cover the mouth of the jar with fabric and secure with a rubber band. Ferment at room temperature until it is actively bubbling, about 1 to 3 days.

**7** Transfer the ginger beer to sterilized bottles and seal. Leave to sit at room temperature for 1 to 4 days (depending on the ambient temperature) before refrigerating. Ginger beer can be stored in the fridge for several months.

**Ginger beer** and ginger ale are not the same! While ginger beer is **a naturally fermented beverage,** ginger ale is simply carbonated water with ginger flavour added.

This sweet and sour beverage is often served over ice in a glass with a chilli and salt rim. It's also a great mixer and pairs perfectly with rum.

**Ferment** Bacterial/Yeast    **Prep** 10 minutes    **Time** 2 to 3 days    **Makes** 3 litres (5¼ pints)

# TEPACHE

This pineapple base can be varied and adapted using different fruit and spice combinations. Try adding tamarind, whole sugar cane pieces, guava, orange slices, or hibiscus flowers.

## ⬇ YOU WILL NEED...

1 whole pineapple

1 large piece solid unrefined sugar cane

1 cinnamon stick

3 to 4 whole cloves

3 litres (5¼ pints) water

4 litre (1 gallon) jar

## ⬇ METHOD

**1** Remove the pineapple rind and cut the fruit from the core. Save the rind and core and set aside the fruit for another use.

**Only the rind and core of the pineapple are used.**

In Mexico, **beer is often added** to tepache, creating a refreshing alcoholic beverage. Try adding a **Mexican lager** to your tepache after the second day of fermenting.

**2** Place the pineapple rind and core in the glass jar.

**4** Cover the mouth of the jar with fabric and secure with a rubber band. Ferment at room temperature for 2 to 3 days. Stir twice a day and taste. When you are satisfied with the level of fermentation, strain the tepache and refrigerate it.

**3** Add the sugar cane, cinnamon, and cloves. Add enough water to cover, leaving 5–7.5cm (2–3in) of headspace at the top of the jar.

Naturally sweet amazake, a Japanese fermented rice, makes an excellent base for a sugar-free horchata. The flavour is light, delicate, and delicious.

**Ferment** Mould    **Prep** 20 minutes    **Time** 20 minutes    **Makes** approx 960ml (1½ pints)

# AMAZAKE HORCHATA

You can make your own amazake or buy it at a specialty store. Try adding a handful of cacao nibs to the blender for a flavour reminiscent of *chilate*, a cacao and rice beverage that is popular in the Mexican state of Guerrero.

 ## YOU WiLL NEED...

400g (14oz) **amazake** (p118)

480ml (15½fl oz) water

½ tsp ground cinnamon

⅛ tsp vanilla powder or extract (optional)

 ## METHOD

**1** In a blender, combine the amazake, water, cinnamon, and vanilla (if using). Blend for between 3 and 5 minutes.

**2** Allow the mixture to rest at room temperature for 20 minutes before serving.

**3** Stir or shake well and serve over ice. Garnish with a sprinkle of cinnamon.

Horchata is often served as a **refreshing breakfast drink** and is considered by some to be a **remedy for hangovers**. Variations of this ancient beverage include using almonds, dates, and even lime zest.

Water kefir is an effervescent, probiotic beverage made from water kefir grains. Once you have activated your water kefir grains, you can use them to make this lacto-fermented beverage using fruit juice or coconut water.

**Ferment** Bacterial     **Prep** 5 minutes     **Time** 1 to 3 days     **Makes** approx 960ml (1½ pints)

# WATER KEFIR

##  YOU WiLL NEED...

50g (1¾oz) hydrated water kefir grains

60g (2oz) unrefined sugar

1 litre (1¾ pints) filtered or spring water, warmed

2 litre (3½ pint) jar

Bottles for bottling

##  METHOD

**1** Remove the water kefir grains from their packaging. If they came in liquid, discard the liquid and rinse the grains.

**2** Using the sterilized jar, dissolve the sugar in the warm water. Allow the water to cool to room temperature and add the kefir grains.

**3** Cover the jar with fabric and a rubber band and leave at room temperature, out of direct sunlight, for 1 to 3 days or until the water kefir is effervescent and tastes pleasantly tart.

**4** Strain the water kefir, reserving the grains, and bottle the liquid. Water kefir will keep, refrigerated, for several weeks.

**5** Use the water kefir grains for another batch immediately or refrigerate in a jar with a small amount of water. Use within 1 month.

Water kefir **grains** are available from online sources and some natural food stores. They resemble **clear jelly-like curds** and may need to be hydrated before using.

A very effective digestive, coconut water kefir has all the benefits of coconut water, plus probiotics. Its light, tart flavour is distinctly different from dairy kefir.

**Ferment** Bacterial/Yeast    **Prep** 5 minutes    **Time** 1 to 2 days    **Makes** approx 480ml (15½fl oz)

# COCONUT WATER KEFIR

## YOU WILL NEED...

480ml (15½fl oz) coconut water (canned or from whole young coconut)

2 tbsp plain **water kefir,** or 2 tbsp activated water kefir grains

1 litre (1¾ pint) jar

Bottles for bottling

Save and refrigerate 60ml (2fl oz) of coconut water kefir to use as the **starter for your next batch.** You can use this starter to make water kefir out of almost any kind of fruit juice.

## METHOD

**1** Pour the coconut water into the sterilized jar. Add the water kefir or water kefir grains and stir.

**2** Cover the mouth of the jar with breathable fabric and secure it with a rubber band.

**3** Ferment for 1 to 2 days at room temperature. Bottle when you are satisfied with the level of fermentation. (If using water kefir grains, strain them out before bottling.) Coconut water kefir will keep, refrigerated, for several weeks.

The digestive enzymes in pineapple and stomach-settling properties of ginger make this an excellent after-meal tonic. It is fresh, fruity, and spicy with a characteristic kefir tanginess.

**Ferment** Bacterial/Yeast    **Prep** 5 minutes    **Time** 2 to 4 days    **Makes** 1 litre (1¾ pints)

# PINEAPPLE
## GINGER KEFIR

Fermenting with pineapple juice requires care. Due to its high sugar content, carbonation can build up quickly in the sealed bottles. Do not let the bottles sit at room temperature for more than 1 to 2 days.

###  YOU WILL NEED...

1 litre (1¾ pints) pineapple juice, either store-bought or homemade

1 tsp fresh root ginger, grated

120ml (4fl oz) **coconut water kefir** (p167)

2 litre (3½ pint) jar

Bottles for bottling

### METHOD

1 Pour the pineapple juice into the sterilized jar. Add the starter liquid and ginger. Stir well to combine.

2 Cover the mouth of the jar with a piece of breathable material, such as muslin, and secure it with a rubber band.

3 Leave to sit at room temperature, away from light, for 1 to 2 days. When you are satisfied with the level of fermentation, transfer to the sterilized bottles.

4 Keep the bottles at room temperature to carbonate for no more than 1 or 2 days before transferring to the fridge.

# STARTING & SHARING SCOBYS

SCOBY stands for "symbiotic colony of bacteria and yeast" and refers to the gelatinous disc that forms on the surface of an active batch of kombucha or jun. You need a SCOBY in order to make kombucha or jun, but luckily they are easy to grow, split, and share with others.

## YOUR FiRST SCOBY

There are several ways to obtain your first SCOBY. The best and easiest option is to get one from a friend or acquaintance who makes kombucha. It's also possible to purchase SCOBYs through speciality stores, or you can grow one yourself. All you need is a bottle of raw, unfiltered kombucha, some freshly brewed tea, sugar, and time.

If **more than four weeks** pass and your SCOBY hasn't formed, the starter kombucha may have been weak or old. **Start fresh** with a new batch.

**Choosing a tea**
Any plain black or green tea will work well, but you can also use white and oolong teas if you like. Herbal teas are not recommended.

1 Brew 500ml (16fl oz) of green or black tea. Add 3 tablespoons of sugar and stir to dissolve. Cool to room temperature.

2 Pour a 500ml (16fl oz) bottle of plain, raw kombucha into a 2-litre (3½-pint) jar. Add the cooled, sweetened tea to the jar and stir to mix.

3 Cover the mouth of the jar with fabric and secure with a rubber band. Ferment at room temperature, away from light, for 1 to 2 weeks.

In a few weeks, a SCOBY should begin to form on the surface of the liquid. The SCOBY that forms and the liquid that remains can then be used to start making kombucha.

The SCOBY will form on the surface of the tea after 1 to 2 weeks.

Keep an extra jar as a "**SCOBY motel**" to house **unneeded SCOBYs** until you can share them.

**SCOBY storage**
Keep your SCOBYs in a covered jar at room temperature. Make sure the SCOBYs are completely submerged in the liquid.

Newer SCOBYs called "daughters" form at the top of the liquid.

Daughter

Daughter

Mother

## A LIVING COLONY

SCOBYs form at the top of the fermentation vessel, where they take on the shape of the surface. They grow in layers, one on top of the other. The newer SCOBYs that form near the surface are called "daughters," while the original SCOBY at the bottom is the "mother."

## WATCH FOR MOULD

As a growing organism, a SCOBY takes on a life of its own, and it may look a little strange at first. You may see small strands of yeast growing from the bottom of the SCOBY, which is normal. However, if you see mould growing on the surface of the SCOBY, you should discard the SCOBY and sterilize all of your equipment.

## SPLITTING SCOBYS

Sometimes the daughters form on top of each other in separate layers, making it very easy to separate them and give them away or use them to start more batches. Alternatively, they may be fused together. In this case, you may have to cut them into smaller pieces. Always use a wooden, plastic, or ceramic knife to split SCOBYs. Do not use metal knives for this.

## SHARING YOUR SCOBYS

As long as they are submerged in the kombucha and don't dry out, your SCOBYs can last for several months. When the time comes to share, cut off a piece of SCOBY and place it in a jar with some kombucha to cover it. It will eventually take on the size and shape of its new home.

This fermented tea drink is made and revered in Russia, China, and Japan. The unique symbiosis of yeast and bacteria makes a delicious and healthful tonic.

**Ferment** Bacterial/Yeast    **Prep** 20 minutes    **Time** 1 to 4 weeks    **Makes** 2 litres (3½ pints)

# KOMBUCHA

Kombucha ferments best in warmer temperatures, between 20–30°C (70–85°F). In the colder months, it can take up to 4 weeks for kombucha to come to maturity. Be patient and move the vessel to a warmer location if needed.

## YOU WiLL NEED...

85g (3oz) loose leaf green or black tea, or 8 to 10 green or black tea bags

2 litres (3½ pints) hot water

85g (3oz) cane sugar

1 SCOBY

120ml (4fl oz) plain kombucha

2 litre (3½ pint) preserving jar

## METHOD

**1** In a large jar, combine the tea and water. Leave to steep for 5 to 10 minutes.

Use a heat-safe vessel for steeping.

Green or black teas are the best choices when making kombucha. **Avoid** using any teas that have **additives or flavourings**, which can impede the fermentation process.

**2** Strain the tea into the sterilized jar, leaving at least 7.5cm (3 in) of headspace.

**Save your spent tea leaves to make Lahpet!**

**3** Add the sugar and stir until dissolved. (The sugar feeds the SCOBY during the fermentation process.)

Continued

Store-bought kombucha comes in many flavours and varieties, but purchase a plain kombucha for starting your homemade batch.

**4** Add the kombucha and stir. This addition will kick-start the fermentation process.

**5** Place the SCOBY on the surface of the liquid. (Don't worry if it sinks at first.)

**6** Cover the mouth of the jar with a piece of fabric and secure with a rubber band. Place in a warm, dark location and leave to sit for 7 to 10 days.

Use a breathable fabric. The SCOBY uses oxygen and expels carbon dioxide during fermentation.

An air-tight seal will preserve the natural effervescence of kombucha.

**7** Bottle and keep at room temperature for 1 to 2 days to carbonate. Refrigerate the bottles when the carbonation is sufficient. Open a bottle carefully and have a glass ready to catch the foam in case of over-carbonation.

Have fun experimenting with different ingredients and techniques, but always brew a **simple "safe" batch** along with your experiment so that you don't lose your starter.

This rosy-hued beverage combines the delicate fruit flavours of cherry and bergamot with the sour effervescence of kombucha for a unique and refreshing drink.

**Ferment** Bacterial/Yeast    **Prep** 1½ hours    **Time** 1 to 4 weeks    **Makes** 2 litres (3½ pints)

# EARL GREY
# CHERRY KOMBUCHA

Other tea varieties can be used in this recipe, but it's best to avoid teas with added flavours or spices that could inhibit or weaken the yeast and bacterial cultures. Additional flavouring can be added in the bottling stage without compromising the SCOBY for future batches.

##  YOU WiLL NEED...

3 tbsp loose Earl Grey tea leaves, or 5 to 8 Earl Grey tea bags

2 litres (3½ pints) boiling water

85g (3oz) cane sugar

1 SCOBY

120ml (4fl oz) plain kombucha (purchased or homemade)

450ml (fl oz) unsweetened cherry juice

2 litre (3½ pint) jar

Bottles for bottling

## METHOD

1 Place the tea in a large, heatproof vessel with a wide mouth. Pour boiling water over the tea. Allow to steep, uncovered, until cooled to room temperature. (This releases much of the bergamot oil, which can inhibit fermentation.)

2 Strain the tea into the jar, leaving at least 7.5cm (3 in) of headspace. Add the sugar and stir until dissolved. Add the kombucha and stir to mix the ingredients well.

3 Place the SCOBY on the surface of the liquid. Cover the mouth of the jar with fabric and secure with rubber bands. Set in a warm, dark place. Ferment for 1 to 4 weeks, depending on the ambient temperature.

4 Once you are satisfied with the level of fermentation, transfer the kombucha to the sterilized bottles, filling each only up to the neck.

5 Top off each bottle with cherry juice, leaving 2.5cm (1in) of headspace.

6 Leave to sit at room temperature for 1 to 3 days (or longer in colder environments) to carbonate before refrigerating. Kombucha will keep, refrigerated, for several months.

Prickly pears give this refreshing Mexican fermented beverage a bright red colour as well as a sweet, berry-like flavour with notes of cucumber.

**Ferment** Bacterial    **Prep** 15 minutes    **Time** 3 to 5 days    **Makes** 3 litres (5¼ pints)

# COLONCHE (FERMENTED PRICKLY PEAR)

## YOU WiLL NEED...

8 to 10 ripe prickly pears

1 large piece of unrefined sugar cane, or 1 cup honey

3 litres (5¼ pints) water

4 litre (1 gallon) jar

Bottles for bottling

## METHOD

**1** In a large bowl, soak the prickly pears in water for 1 hour to soften their thorns. Pour off the water and tumble the pears in the bowl to loosen the thorns. Rinse the prickly pears thoroughly and slice them in half.

**2** Add the prickly pears and sugar cane or honey to the jar. Add enough water to cover. Cover the mouth of the jar with breathable fabric and secure with a rubber band.

**3** Leave to sit at room temperature, away from direct sunlight, for 3 to 5 days. Stir twice a day to encourage yeast activity.

**4** When you are happy with the level of fermentation, strain the liquid through muslin (to remove any lingering thorns) and bottle.

This drink is traditionally made with **Piloncillo** (also known as panela), a type of sugar that is commonly sold in Mexican markets in the shape of **cones or blocks**.

Jun is a fermented tea with a pleasantly sweet-and-sour taste and slight effervesence. Like kombucha, each new batch of jun is made using a small amount of jun from a previous batch.

**Ferment** Bacterial/Yeast   **Prep** 20 minutes   **Time** 1 to 4 weeks   **Makes** 2 litres (3½ pints)

# JUN (FERMENTED TEA WITH HONEY)

 ## YOU WiLL NEED...

50g (1¾oz) loose leaf green tea, or 8 to 10 green tea bags

2 litres (3½ pints) water warmed to approx 49°C /170°F

175g (6oz) honey

120ml (4fl oz) plain jun (homemade or purchased)

1 SCOBY

2 litre (3½ pint) jar

Bottles for bottling

## METHOD

1 Place the tea in a large, heatproof vessel with a wide mouth. Pour the warmed water over the tea and steep for 15 minutes.

2 Strain the tea into the jar, leaving at least 7.5cm (3in) headspace. Add the honey and stir until dissolved. Once the sweet tea has cooled to lukewarm, add the jun and stir to mix.

3 Place the SCOBY on the surface of the liquid. Cover the mouth of the jar with a piece of fabric and secure with a rubber band. Set in a warm, dark place and ferment for 1 to 4 weeks, depending on the ambient temperature.

4 Once you are satisfied with the level of fermentation, transfer to the sterilized bottles and seal.

5 Leave to sit at room temperature for 1 to 3 days (longer in colder environments) to carbonate before refrigerating. Jun will keep, refrigerated, for several months.

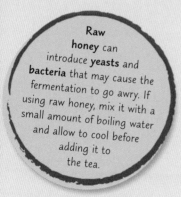
Raw honey can introduce yeasts and bacteria that may cause the fermentation to go awry. If using raw honey, mix it with a small amount of boiling water and allow to cool before adding it to the tea.

This Eastern European tonic has a ruby colour and an earthy, slightly salty flavour. It is an amazing digestive and delivers the blood-cleansing benefits of beetroot.

**Ferment** Bacterial/Yeast    **Prep** 10 minutes    **Time** 3 to 14 days    **Makes** 1 litre (1¾ pints)

# BEETROOT KVASS

Beetroot kvass can be consumed on its own as a tangy and nutritious tonic or added to dressings and dips for a nutrient boost and reddish hue. It will also brighten both the colour and flavour of *borscht*, a traditional Ukrainian beetroot soup.

##  YOU WILL NEED...

3 medium beetroots

2 to 3 tsp salt

1 litre (1¾ pints) water

1 litre (1¾ pint) jar

Bottles for bottling

##  METHOD

**1** Chop the beetroots into 1.25cm (½-in) cubes and place in the jar.

**2** Add the salt and enough water to completely cover all the beetroot.

**3** Cover loosely with a lid and ferment at room temperature for at least 3 days before tasting. The longer you allow it to ferment, the tangier the kvass will become.

**4** When you are happy with the level of fermentation, transfer the kvass to sterilized bottles and seal, reserving the beetroots in the jar for any additional batches.

To make additional batches of kvass, add **more salt and water** to the same beetroots. The beetroots should be discarded after making three batches.

This tangy and creamy fermented beverage is made from coconut milk. It's an excellent dairy-free alternative to milk kefir, with all the same probiotic benefits.

**Ferment** Bacterial/Yeast    **Prep** 30 minutes    **Time** 1 to 3 days    **Makes** approx 750ml (1¼ pints)

# COCONUT MILK KEFIR

Coconut milk, which is extracted from the white flesh of the coconut, is different from coconut water, the liquid found in the centre of the coconut. When extracting the milk, process it as finely as possible to ensure that all of the liquid is captured.

## ⬇ YOU WiLL NEED...

750ml (1¼ pints) hot water

200g (7oz) unsweetened shredded coconut

60ml (2fl oz) **water kefir** (p166)

1 litre (1¾ pints) jar

## ⬇ METHOD

**1** In a blender or food processor, combine the hot water and shredded coconut. Blend on high for 4 to 5 minutes.

The **coconut pulp** left over from making coconut milk is a wonderful by-product that can be used for **baking**.

To expel as much liquid as possible, gather the corners of the fabric into a tight ball and squeeze.

**2** In a colander lined with muslin or cheesecloth, strain the coconut mix, pressing to extract all the liquid. Set aside the pulp to use in other recipes or dehydrate for future use.

**3** Transfer the fresh coconut milk to the sterilized jar and cool to room temperature. Add the water kefir and stir to combine.

**4** Cover the mouth of jar with fabric and secure with a rubber band. Ferment for 1 to 3 days, depending on the ambient temperature. When the kefir is tart and creamy, refrigerate. Kefir will keep, refrigerated, for several weeks.

# ALCOHOL

Alcoholic beverages are some of the earliest and most ubiquitous forms of fermentation. Take part in this tradition by brewing your own cider, ginger beer, mead, and much more, at home.

This bracing ginger beer has the same spicy, citrusy flavour as the non-alcoholic version, but the larger quantity of sugar and longer fermentation time result in an alcoholic beverage.

**Ferment** Yeast    **Prep** 45 minutes    **Time** 2 weeks    **Makes** 3 650ml (22fl oz) bottles

# HARD GINGER BEER

The world of botanically brewed ginger beer is a vast one, and there are many herbs you can add to the boiling water along with the ginger. Some delicious options include lemongrass, allspice, cinnamon, cloves, kaffir lime leaves, citrus peel, juniper berries, and dandelion root.

## YOU WiLL NEED...

- 2.5–7.5cm (1–3in) fresh root ginger, grated or sliced
- 2 litres (3½ pints) water
- 200g (7oz) sugar, plus ¾ teaspoon for bottling
- Juice of 1 small lemon or 2 limes
- 3 tbsp **ginger bug** (p156), strained
- 4 litre (1 gallon) demijohn and airlock
- 3 650ml (22fl oz) bottles

## METHOD

1 In a saucepan, bring the ginger and 1 litre (1¾ pints) of water to a boil over a high heat. Boil for 15 minutes.

2 Using a funnel and sieve, strain and transfer the ginger infusion to the sterilized demijohn. Do not discard the ginger.

3 Return the ginger to the saucepan and add the remaining 1 litre (1¾ pints) of water. Bring to a boil over a high heat and then boil for 15 minutes.

4 Strain the second batch of ginger infusion into the demijohn. (The ginger can be saved for another use or discarded.)

5 Add the sugar to the demijohn and swirl to dissolve. Leave to cool to room temperature.

6 Add the ginger bug and lemon or lime juice to the demijohn. Attach the airlock and ferment at room temperature for 2 weeks. The ginger beer should begin bubbling within 24 hours.

7 Bottle the ginger beer into the sterilized bottles, leaving 5cm (2in) of headspace at the top of each bottle. Add ¼ teaspoon sugar to each bottle and seal.

8 To carbonate, keep the bottles at room temperature for 2 to 4 weeks (depending on the ambient temperature) before refrigerating.

Like its namesake, this kefir beverage is tart, dry, and highly effervescent.
It's perfect for celebratory toasts or as a stand-in for sparkling wine in
Buck's Fizz and other cocktails.

**Ferment** Lacto & Yeast    **Prep** 5 minutes    **Time** 5 to 7 days    **Makes** 2 litres (3½ pints)

# KEFIR CHAMPAGNE

Any fruit juice can be used in this recipe, but juices with a high sugar
content, such as pineapple, will ferment more readily. Water kefir
can create powerful carbonation, so use thick, high-quality glass
bottles that can handle the pressure. Be careful when opening the
bottles, and don't let them carbonate for more than two weeks.

## YOU WiLL NEED...

2 litres (3½ pints) pineapple juice

120ml **water kefir** (p166)

4 litre (1 gallon) demijohn and
  airlock

Bottles for bottling

## METHOD

**1** Pour the juice and water kefir into the demijohn. Swirl around
to combine. Attach the airlock and leave to sit at room
temperature for 5 to 7 days.

**2** When the kefir only has a slight amount of sweetness left,
transfer to the sterilized bottles, leaving behind the lees, or yeast
sediment, in the demijohn. (The lees can be discarded.) Leave 5cm
(2in) headspace.

**3** Let the bottles sit at room temperature for 1 to 2 weeks,
depending on the ambient temperature and the sweetness of the
kefir at the time of bottling. If it is warm or you have bottled it while
still quite sweet, it could carbonate more quickly than expected.

**4** Transfer the bottles to the fridge and keep refrigerated for 1 to 2
months to allow the flavours to balance. Make sure each bottle
is well-chilled before opening.

This crisp and tart alcoholic beverage is a perfect autumn fermenting project. It can be made with juice from any variety of apple, or use pear juice to make perry.

**Ferment** Yeast   **Prep** 15 minutes   **Time** 2 months   **Makes** 4 litres (7 pints)

# HARD CIDER

The champagne yeast called for in this recipe is a strain that can be purchased online or at any homebrewing supply store. Do not use baker's yeast, which is not intended for brewing.

## YOU WiLL NEED...

4 litres (7 pints) freshly pressed sweet cider, or unfiltered apple juice

¼ pack champagne yeast (about ¼ tsp)

2 4-litre (1-gallon) demijohns and airlocks

Bottles for bottling

## METHOD

**1** In a small jar, mix the yeast with 120ml (4fl oz) of apple juice that is at room temperature. Cover and set aside for 30 minutes.

Mixing the yeast with a small amount of apple juice will activate it.

At each stage of the cider brewing process, be sure to **clean and sterilize** any equipment that comes into contact with the juice or cider, including **funnels**, **demijohns**, and **bottles**.

A metal funnel is less likely to harbour bacteria than one made from plastic.

**2** Reserve 500ml (16fl oz) of apple juice and pour the rest into the sterilized demijohn using a sterilized funnel. Freeze the reserved apple juice for bottle conditioning later.

**3** Add the activated yeast liquid to the demijohn.

Continued ⬛▷

If you juice your own apples, **strain out the pulp** before transfering the cider to the **second demijohn**. A large muslin or nylon "brew bag" can be used for straining.

The spent yeast will form a yeast cake at the bottom of the demijohn.

**4** Cork the demijohn with an airlock and leave to sit in a cool place out of direct sunlight for 2 weeks. During this time, the cider will bubble with active fermentation.

**5** After fermentation slows, gently transfer the cider to another clean, 4-litre (1-gallon) glass demijohn, leaving behind the settled yeast particulate. Try not to disturb the settled yeast during the transfer. Insert the airlock. Leave at room temperature for 4 weeks.

**Be sure to leave adequate headspace for the reserved apple juice to be added.**

**6** Once the active fermentation (bubbling) has completely stopped, transfer the cider to glass bottles, leaving 7.5cm (3in) of headspace.

**7** Top off each bottle with a little defrosted reserved apple juice, leaving 5cm (2in) of headspace and seal. Let the bottles sit at room temperature for 2 weeks to carbonate before transferring to the fridge.

**Using unprocessed (unpasteurized) apple juice will result in a cloudy cider.**

Cider can be aged; however, fermenting for **longer than a month** will result in a **less sweet** and **more wine-like** beverage that may have "off" flavours.

This winter favourite combines the fragrant, warming spices of cinnamon, cloves, and allspice with hard cider. Serve warm and enjoy around an open fire.

**Ferment** Yeast    **Prep** 30 minutes    **Time** 2 months    **Makes** 3 litres (5¼ pints)

# SPICED HARD CIDER

## YOU WiLL NEED...

4 litres (7 pints) unfiltered apple juice, or freshly pressed sweet cider

¼ pack champagne yeast (about ¼ tsp.)

1 cinnamon stick

3 whole cloves

2 allspice berries

2 4-litre (1-gallon) demijohns and airlocks

Bottles for bottling

## METHOD

**1** To activate the yeast, mix it with 120ml (4fl oz) apple juice (at room temperature). Cover and set aside for 30 minutes.

**2** Reserve 500ml (16fl oz) of apple juice and pour the rest of the juice into the sterilized demijohn using a sterilized funnel. Freeze the reserved apple juice for bottle conditioning later on.

**3** Add the activated yeast to carboy. Cork with an airlock and leave to sit in a cool place, away from light, for 2 weeks. After a few days, signs of fermentation (bubbling) should be evident.

**4** Once fermentation slows, transfer the cider to a second sterilized demijohn, leaving behind the settled yeast. Attach an airlock and leave for 4 more weeks or until bubbling has ceased.

**5** In a saucepan, combine reserved defrosted apple juice, cinnamon stick, cloves, and allspice. Bring to a simmer over a medium-high heat and simmer for 15 minutes. Cool to room temperature.

**6** Transfer the fermented cider to the sterilized bottles, filling just up to the neck. Top off each bottle with the spiced reserved apple juice, leaving 5cm (2in) headspace.

**7** Seal the bottles and leave to sit at room temperature for at least 2 weeks to carbonate.

Mead, or honey wine, dates back to ancient times. The honey used for mead will affect the final flavour profile, so select a honey you enjoy. The long fermentation time will yield a lightly sweet, straw-coloured wine.

**Ferment** Yeast     **Prep** 15 minutes     **Time** 6 to 12 months     **Makes** 4 litres (1 gallon)

# MEAD

##  YOU WiLL NEED...

¼ tsp champagne yeast

1kg (2¼lb) honey

3 litres (5¼ pints) water

2 4-litre (1-gallon) demijohns and airlocks

Bottles for bottling

##  METHOD

**1** To activate the yeast, mix it with 120ml (4fl oz) of water (at room temperature) and leave to sit for 15 minutes.

**2** Combine the honey, water, and activated yeast in the sterilized demijohn. Swirl or shake well to dissolve the honey.

**3** Attach the airlock to the demijohn. Leave to sit at room temperature, away from light, for 1 to 2 months or until the bubbling has stopped and active fermentation has ceased.

**4** Gently transfer the mead to another sterilized demijohn, leaving behind the yeast sediment, which can be discarded.

**5** Attach an airlock to the new demijohn and allow it to ferment for another month or until all signs of fermentation have ceased.

**6** Bottle and store in a cool place. Allow the mead to age for at least 6 months. Longer ageing will yield better results.

Traditionally, mead was made by **mixing raw honey and water** and allowing the **wild yeasts** in the honey to proliferate.

This ruby-coloured mead includes the raspberry leaf as well as the fruit, delivering the flavour and medicinal qualities of the whole plant.

**Ferment** Yeast    **Prep** 1 hour    **Time** 6 to 12 months    **Makes** 4 litres (1 gallon)

# RASPBERRY MEAD

##  YOU WiLL NEED...

3 litres (5¼ pints), plus 120ml (4fl oz) water

55g (2oz) dried raspberry leaves

¼ tsp champagne yeast

1kg (2¼lb) honey

200g (7oz) fresh raspberries

2 4-litre (1-gallon) demijohns and airlocks

Bottles for bottling

## METHOD

**1** In a large pot, combine 3 litres (5¼ pints) of the water and dried raspberry leaves. Bring to a boil over high heat and boil for 15 minutes. Set aside and cool to room temperature.

**2** To activate the yeast, mix it with the remaining water (at room temperature) and leave to sit for 15 minutes.

**3** Strain the raspberry leaf tea and combine with the honey and raspberries in the sterilized demijohn. Cool to room temperature.

**4** Add the activated yeast to the demijohn and attach an airlock. Leave to sit at room temperature, away from light, for 1 to 2 months or until active fermentation has ceased.

**5** Rack the raspberry mead by straining out the fruit and transferring the liquid to another sterilized demijohn. Attach an airlock and allow it to ferment for 1 month or until there are no signs of fermentation.

**6** Bottle the raspberry mead and store in a cool place. Allow it to age for at least 6 months. Longer ageing will yield better results.

# CUSTOMIZING YOUR BREWS

Once you have the basics of making fermented beverages, you can add your own unique expression to them by varying colours and flavours.

Colouring and flavouring additions can be added at different points in the fermentation process, depending on the result you desire. Add to the fermentation vessel during primary fermentation for maximum extraction, or during secondary fermentation for a lighter infusion.

## COLOUR ADDITIONS

Depending on the colouring agent, there are many ways to incorporate colour. Try using juices, powders, concentrates, and/or whole ingredients.

**Green**
- Chlorella • Spirulina • Spinach
- Matcha • Wheatgrass

**Adding green**
Greens can turn to brown in an acidic environment, so add them at the end of fermentation or just before serving for the most vibrant results.

**Orange**
- Carrot
- Calendula
- Paprika

**Yellow**
- Turmeric
- Chrysanthemum

**Purple**
- Blueberry
- Blackberry
- Mulberry
- Red cabbage

**Red**
- Hibiscus
- Pomegranate
- Beetroot
- Raspberry

# FLAVOUR ADDITIONS

Fresh or dried herbs and spices added during secondary fermentation are said to be "dry hopped" and will produce a more aromatic result. You can also use herbs and spices to make an herbal syrup, which can be added to your brew before bottling. This will also help to prime the bottles for carbonation.

### Bittering
- Dandelion
  (flower, leaf, and root)
- Artichoke leaf
- Gentian root
- Oregon grape root
- Burdock
- Sweet flag (calamus)

Bitter herbs such as dandelion can aid in digestion.

### Sweetening
- Licorice root
- Anise seed
- Cinnamon
- Stevia

Sweetening agents like cinnamon will balance bitter flavours.

### Floral
- Orange blossoms
- Chamomile
- Rose
- Jasmine
- Lavender

Use delicate floral additions like lavendar in lighter brews.

### Aromatic
- Coriander seeds
- Cardamom
- Juniper berry
- Orange peel
- Lemon peel
- Cloves
- Allspice
- Nutmeg

Orange peel and other aromatics have preservative properties.

### Spicy
- Dried chillies
- Black peppercorns
- Ginger

Warming spices like chillies can increase circulation.

### Fresh
- Spearmint
- Peppermint
- Rosemary
- Lemon balm
- Lemon verbena
- Lemongrass

Rosemary adds a refreshing note to summer beverages.

This country wine is very similar to sherry in its sweetness and mouthfeel. It is delicious as a dessert wine or can be used in craft cocktails.

**Ferment** Yeast    **Prep** 45 minutes    **Time** 2 to 4 weeks    **Makes** 3 litres (5¼ pints)

# MANDARIN WINE

If you have access to fresh orange blossoms, adding them to the fermentation vessel will impart a heavenly aroma to the brew. If orange blossoms are not available, you can experiment with any fragrant edible flower.

##  YOU WILL NEED...

¼ tsp champagne yeast, or 3 to 4 tbsp **ginger bug** (p156)

3 litres (5¼ pints) mandarin or tangerine juice

800g (1¾lb) sugar

2 4-litre (1-gallon) demijohns and airlocks

Bottles for bottling

## METHOD

**1** In a small jar, mix the yeast with 120ml (4fl oz) of mandarin juice (at room temperature). Leave to sit for 15 minutes.

**2** Combine the remaining mandarin juice and sugar in a sterilized demijohn.

**3** Add the activated yeast to the demijohn and attach an airlock. Leave to sit in a cool place, away from light, for 2 weeks.

**4** After active fermentation has subsided, rack the wine by transferring it to the other sterilized demijohn, leaving the lees (yeast sediment) behind. (The lees can be discarded.)

**5** Attach an airlock and ferment for 2 more weeks or until all signs of fermentation have ceased.

**6** Bottle and age for at least 1 month. Longer ageing will result in a richer, more balanced wine.

Sato is the Thai word for rice wine, a beverage that exists in many forms throughout Asia. It has a strong, somewhat fruity flavour and is best served cold.

**Ferment** Yeast     **Prep** 30 minutes     **Time** 1 to 2 months     **Makes** approx 1 litre (1¾ pints)

# SATO

Jiuqu, or Shanghai yeast balls, contain both the yeast that aids fermentation as well as mould that breaks down the starches in rice to simple sugars. They can be found in Asian shops.

## YOU WiLL NEED...

1.35kg (3lb) cooked glutinous, sticky, or sweet rice

4 jiuqu (Shanghai yeast balls, Chinese rice wine starter)

4 litre (1 gallon) wide-mouth jar

Bottles for bottling

## METHOD

1 With a pestle and mortar or the back of a spoon, crush the yeast balls into a powdery consistency. (You may need to run them through a fine sieve.)

2 Add the rice to the sterilized jar in thin layers, sprinkling yeast ball powder evenly through a sieve over the surface of each layer. Cover the mouth of the jar with fabric and secure with a rubber band.

3 Leave to sit at room temperature, away from light, for 1 to 2 weeks. Stir at least once a day, until the rice begins to take on a liquid-like consistency.

4 Strain and bottle immediately for a light sato, or transfer to a sterilized demijohn with an airlock to further ferment for another 1 to 2 weeks before bottling it.

5 For the best flavour, refrigerate the bottles and let the sato age for another month in the fridge.

This strong, full-bodied sweet wine is reminiscent of port or sherry. It can be sipped in small amounts after a meal or mixed with sparkling water or spirits.

**Ferment** Yeast   **Prep** 5 minutes   **Time** 6 to 12 months   **Makes** 2 litres (3½ pints)

# DATE WINE

Give this wine time. The strong flavours created during fermentation may not be appealing right away. After 1 to 2 years of ageing, however, the flavour will become balanced and smooth.

## YOU WILL NEED...

¼ tsp champagne yeast, or 3 tbsp
   **ginger bug** (p156)

750g (1⅓ lb) pitted dates

2 litres (3½ pints) water

4 litre (1 gallon) wide-mouth jar

4 litre (1 gallon) demijohn and
   airlock

## METHOD

1 If using yeast, mix it with 120ml (4fl oz) of water (at room temperature) in a small jar. Leave to sit for 15 minutes.

2 Loosely pack the dates into the wide-mouth jar, leaving at least 5cm (2in) of headspace.

3 Add the activated yeast or ginger bug to the jar, followed by enough water to cover the dates. Cover the mouth of the jar with fabric and secure with a rubber band.

4 Leave to sit at room temperature, away from light, for 2 weeks. Stir once a day or until it stops bubbling and active fermentation ceases.

5 Rack the date wine by straining it and transferring all the liquid to a a sterilized demijohn with an airlock.

6 Ferment for 1 month and then bottle. Date wine will be drinkable immediately, but benefits from at least 1 year of ageing.

# VINEGAR

Fermented vinegars are healthy, versatile creations that are limited only by the ingredients in your kitchen. This chapter includes simple vinegar recipes that use everyday ingredients, as well as instructions for making your own herbal vinegars and a health-boosting "fire cider" tonic.

Use this strong and flavourful vinegar as you would apple cider vinegar. It's an excellent tenderizer and well suited for marinades and dressings.

**Ferment** Bacterial/Yeast    **Prep** 10 minutes    **Time** 2 to 3 weeks    **Makes** 1–2 litres (1¾–3½ pints)

# PINEAPPLE
# CIDER VINEGAR

Much like alcohol, vinegar benefits from at least a few months of ageing. To age, seal the vinegar bottles tightly and keep in a cool dark place. For longer ageing, use bottles made of dark glass and dip the sealed top of the bottle in wax.

##  YOU WiLL NEED...

Core and rind of 1 pineapple

200g (7oz) sugar (optional)

2 litres (3½ pints) water

4 litre (1 gallon) jar

Bottles for bottling

##  METHOD

**1** Coarsely chop the pineapple core and rind and place in the sterilized jar. Add sugar (if using) and enough water to cover.

**2** Cover the mouth of the jar with fabric and secure with a rubber band. Leave to sit at room temperature, away from light, for 2 to 3 weeks. Stir daily to aerate.

**3** When the ferment becomes strongly acidic and vinegary, strain the liquid into sterilized bottles and store in a dark place. Vinegar will keep for 1 to 2 years. For longer ageing, make sure the bottles are filled to the top and completely airtight.

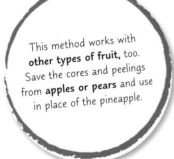

This method works with **other types of fruit,** too. Save the cores and peelings from **apples or pears** and use in place of the pineapple.

Use this versatile vinegar in salad dressings or add a splash to soups and stews for brightness and flavour. Any red wine can be used, but each variety will lend its own flavour.

**Ferment** Bacterial    **Prep** 5 minutes    **Time** 1 to 2 weeks    **Makes** 1 litres (1¾ pints)

# RED WINE VINEGAR

The gelatinous disc that forms on the surface of the liquid during fermentation is the vinegar "mother". It can be reused indefinitely to make more batches of vinegar and will grow and multiply with each batch.

## YOU WiLL NEED...

1 bottle red wine (any variety)

240ml (8fl oz) apple cider vinegar

4 litre (1 gallon) jar

Bottles for bottling

## METHOD

1 Combine the wine and apple cider vinegar in the sterilized jar. Cover the mouth of the jar with breathable fabric and secure with a rubber band.

2 Ferment at room temperature, away from light, for 1 to 2 weeks. Stir daily to aerate.

3 Once all traces of alcohol are gone and only the taste of vinegar remains, remove the "mother" and bottle the vinegar.

4 Store in a dark cupboard. Vinegar will keep for 1 to 2 years in a completely airtight bottle.

Always use **unpasteurized vinegar**. Pasteurized vinegar has been heated to kill any **bad bacteria**, but the process also kills all good bacteria, and pasteurized vinegar will not ferment.

# MAKING HERBAL
# VINEGARS

Not only does unpasteurized vinegar have its own healthful benefits, it's also an amazing solvent for making herbal vinegars, which have long been used in traditional herbal medicine to lessen the symptoms of many common ailments.

## MAKING AN ACETRACT

To make an herbal vinegar, or *acetract*, simply pack the herbs tightly into a jar and add enough vinegar to fully submerge them. After 2 to 4 weeks, the acetract will be ready. Strain the liquid and store it in a dark-coloured bottle and in a dark place. It will keep at room temperature for 1 to 2 years.

## MAKING AN OXYMEL

To soften the flavour of an acetract, make an *oxymel* by adding honey to the finished acetract. Both acetracts and oxymels can be consumed in 1 to 3 tablespoon portions, or added to juice or sparkling water.

**NOTE:** Herbs may or may not help relieve symptoms. Consult with a healthcare professional concerning the treatment of any illness.

## TRADITIONAL HERBS FOR COMMON AILMENTS

### Cold and flu

These herbs may help boost the immune system and lessen cold and flu symptoms, such as sore throat and congestion.

- Echinacea
- Elderberry
- Oregano
- Lemon
- Loquat leaf
- Cayenne
- Yarrow
- Oregon grape root
- Hyssop
- Thyme

### Digestive

For relief for minor digestive disorders such as indigestion or sour stomach, try a vinegar tonic with these herbs.

- Ginger
- Coriander
- Orange peel
- Dandelion
- Peppermint
- Calamus
- Chamomile
- Cardamom
- Cloves
- Fennel
- Wormwood

Elderberry

Peppermint

**Beetroot greens**
Beetroot greens may lower blood pressure and reduce inflammation.

**Echinacea**
Echinacea is believed to be effective in treating colds and urinary tract infections.

**Cloves**
Cloves contains beneficial antioxidant compounds.

## Allergy or inflammation

These herbs may offer temporary relief from allergy symptoms, such as sneezing or itchy eyes, or reduce general inflammation in the body.

- Nettles
- Turmeric
- Milk thistle
- Licorice
- Eyebright
- Feverfew
- Yarrow
- Local honey
- Local bee pollen

## Cleanse

These plants have detoxifying properites that help to cleanse the liver and gallbladder, and promote overall health.

- Beetroot greens
- Coriander
- Parsley
- Dandelion
- Burdock
- Yellow dock
- Milk thistle
- English plantain
- Red clover

## Stress Relief and Relaxation

To reduce stress and promote an improved state of relaxation, try a tonic with these herbal additions.

- Valerian
- Passionflower
- Chamomile
- Lemon balm
- Lavender
- Damiana
- Motherwort
- Mugwort
- Hops

**Turmeric**

**Dandelion**

**Hops**

Infused vinegars are easy to make and impart the flavour of the herbs and spices to the finished product. In this version, the mild sweetness of fennel and tarragon pair with the savoury notes of garlic and onion.

**Ferment** Bacterial    **Prep** 15 minutes    **Time** 2 to 8 weeks    **Makes** approx 500ml (16fl oz)

# INFUSED VINEGAR

The aromatic herbs and spices can remain in the vinegar for a year or more. You can also remove them and use them as a tasty pickled flavouring for soups, stews, or other savoury dishes.

 **YOU WiLL NEED...**

2 cloves garlic

¼ bulb fresh fennel root

1 stalk fresh lemongrass

4 to 5 spring onions

2 tbsp black peppercorns

4 to 5 sprigs fresh tarragon

350ml (12fl oz) unpasteurized apple cider vinegar

1 litre (1¾ pint) jar

 **METHOD**

**1** Slice the garlic, fennel root, lemongrass, and spring onions into uniform pieces.

**2** Place the peppercorns and garlic in the sterilized jar.

**3** Add the fennel, tarragon, lemongrass, and spring onions to the jar.

**4** Pour vinegar over the vegetables to cover, leaving 2.5cm (1in) of headspace at the top of the jar.

The aromatics will become pickled and can be used to flavour soups or salads.

**5** Cover the jar tightly with the lid. Leave to sit at room temperature, away from light, for at least 2 weeks before using. The herbs can be left in or removed and used for another purpose.

White wine vinegar and champagne vinegar can also be infused. Avoid using balsamic vinegar, as its strong flavour may not mix well with the herbs.

This boldly spiced infused vinegar has many restorative health benefits. Sprinkle over salads, rice, or meats for a peppery kick, or get your daily dose by consuming a tablespoon straight as a "shot".

**Ferment** Bacterial  **Prep** 15 minutes  **Time** 6 to 8 weeks  **Makes** approx 500ml (16fl oz)

# FIRE CIDER

This is an extremely adaptable recipe that can be modified to suit your tastes and available ingredients. Replace the thyme with oregano, marjoram, or mint. Add fresh horseradish root for a spicier infusion that targets the respiratory system. If fresh turmeric is not available, substitute with turmeric powder or more ginger.

> Fire cider has long been believed to **strengthen the immune system** and fend off numerous ailments. Taken straight, it **packs a powerful punch** to clear congested sinuses.

 ## YOU WiLL NEED...

1 lemon, quartered with peel

¼ white onion, chopped

6 cloves garlic, sliced

5cm (2in) piece fresh root ginger, chopped

5cm (2in) piece fresh turmeric root, chopped

4 tbsp fresh thyme or 2 tbsp dried thyme

1 to 2 sprigs fresh rosemary

1 to 2 chillies, such as jalapeño, cayenne, or habanero (optional)

350ml (12fl oz) unpasteurized apple cider vinegar

2 to 4 tbsp unpasteurized honey (optional)

1 litre (1¾ pint) jar

 ## METHOD

**1** Pack the lemon quarters, onion, garlic, ginger, turmeric, thyme, and chillies (if using), into the sterilized jar.

**2** Add the apple cider vinegar to the jar, leaving 2.5cm (1in) of headspace at the top.

**3** Cover tightly with the lid and infuse at room temperature, away from light, for 6 to 8 weeks.

**4** Strain the vinegar and bottle. For a milder flavour, add the honey (optional) before bottling and mix well to dissolve. Fire cider can be stored at room temperature.

# INDEX

## A

acetract, 212–213
ageing sauerkraut, 49
aioli
    Spicy aioli, 76
    Vegan aioli, 76
alcoholic beverages
    customizing, 198–199
    Date wine, 204–205
    Hard cider, 190–193
    Hard ginger beer, 186–187
    ideal environment, 25
    Kefir champagne, 188–189
    Mandarin wine, 200–201
    Mead, 196
    Raspberry mead, 197
    Sato, 202–203
    Spiced hard cider, 194–195
allergies, herbal remedies, 213
Amazake, 118–119
    Amazake horchata, 164–165
    Purple amazake sourdough,
      152–153
Amazake horchata, 164–165
American (slicing) cucumbers, 30
apples
    adding to sauerkraut, 46
    Fire cider, 216
    Hard cider, 190–193
    Spiced hard cider, 194–195
aromatic flavours, beverages, 199
asafoetida powder, 51
aubergine, Pickled aubergine, 65
avocadoes, Creamy avocado
  dip, 76

## B

bacteria
    beneficial, 14–15
    SCOBY (Symbiotic Colony Of
      Bacteria and Yeast), 170–171
bacterial ferments, 16–17
beans. **See** legumes
beer, 17
    fermentation, 10
    Ginger beer, 160–161
Beetroot kvass, 180–181
beetroots
    Beetroot kvass, 180–181
    greens, 213
    Lift (Egyptian pickled turnips),
    36–37
    Root kraut, 52–53
beneficial bacteria, 14–15
beverages
    alcoholic
      Date wine, 204–205
      Hard cider, 190–193
      Hard ginger beer, 186–187
      Kefir champagne, 188–189
      Mandarin wine, 200–201
      Mead, 196
      Raspberry mead, 197
      Sato, 202–203
      Spiced hard cider, 194–195
    bottling, 158–159
    carbonating, 158–159
    customizing, 198–199
    non-alcoholic
      Amazake horchata, 164–165
      Beetroot kvass, 180–181
      Coconut milk kefir, 182–183
      Coconut water kefir, 167
      Colonche, 178
      Earl Grey cherry
       Kombucha, 176–177
      Ginger beer, 160–161
      Ginger bug, 156
      Herbal syrup, 157
      Jun, 179
      Kombucha, 172–175
      Pineapple ginger kefir,
       168–169
      Tepache, 162–163
      Water kefir, 166
    SCOBY (Symbiotic Colony Of
      Bacteria and Yeast), 170–171
bittering beverages, 199
blue cheese, 16
Pak choi white kimchi, 60–61
bottling
    beverages, 158–159
    brine, 32
bread
    Buckwheat pancakes, 142–143
    Dosa, 120–123
    Gorditas, 138–139
    Injera, 140–141
    Purple amazake sourdough,
      152–153
    Sourdough bread, 146–149
    Sourdough pizza, 150–151
brie, 16
brine, bottling, 32
Buckwheat pancakes, 142–143
Burmese pickled tea leaves
 (Lahpet), 66–67
butter
    cultured, 94–95
    ghee, 95
buttermilk, cultured, 96–97

## C

cabbage
    Curtido, 54–55
    Kimchi, 56–59
    Masala kraut, 51
    Sauerkraut, 46–49
    Seaweed sauerkraut, 50
Cake icing, 76

carbonating beverages, 158–159
carrots
    adding to sauerkraut, 46
    Continuous pickle, 32
    Turmeric & carrot pickles, 33
Cashew spread, 84–85
    Creamy avocado dip, 76
    Vegan aioli, 76
celeriac (celery root), Root kraut,
  52–53
celery, Continuous pickle, 32
ceramic water crocks, 21
champagne vinegar, infusion, 215
channels, ceramic crocks, 21
cheese
    blue, 16
    brie, 16
    Chevre, 110–111
    equipment, 106–107
    fermentation, 11
    Labneh, 108–109
    Queso fresco, 112–113
    varieties, 107
chef's knives, 39
Chevre, 110–111
Chipotle ketchup, 72
chutneys
    Coconut chutney, 90–91
    Tamarind date chutney, 87
clothespins, 106
cloves, 213
coarse chops, 39
coarse grates, 63
Cocktail sauce, 76
Coco jack tool, 88
Coconut chocolate pudding, 76
Coconut chutney, 90–91
Coconut milk kefir, 182–183
Coconut water kefir, 167
coconuts
    Coconut chutney, 90–91
    Coconut water kefir, 167
    Cultured coconut cream,
      88–89

Cake icing, 76
Coconut chocolate pudding,
  76
colanders, 107
cold and flu herbal remedies, 212
Colonche, 178
colours additions, beverages, 198
condiments
    Cashew spread, 84–85
    Chipotle ketchup, 72
    Classic ketchup, 70–71
    Classic mustard, 74–75
    Cocktail sauce, 76
    Coconut chutney, 90–91
    Cultured coconut cream,
      88–89
    Dijon mustard, 79
    Fresh salsa, 76
    Honey mustard, 76
    Horseradish sauce, 73
    Jalapeño hot sauce, 80–81
    Kimchi, 56–59
    Mole ketchup, 72
    Red horseradish, 76
    Sauerkraut mustard, 78
    Spicy aioli, 76
    Sweet onion relish, 86
    Tamarind date chutney, 87
    uses, 76–77
    Vegan aioli, 76
    Wild habanero hot sauce,
      82–83
Continuous pickle, 32
corn
    Gorditas, 138–139
    Nixtamal, 134–135
Creamy avocado dip, 76
Creamy horseradish salad
  dressing, 76
crocks, ceramic, 21
cucumbers
    Pickling, 30–31
    Japanese pickled cucumber
      (sunomono), 40–41
Cultured butter, 94–95

Cultured buttermilk, 96–97
    Buckwheat pancakes, 142–143
Cultured coconut cream, 88–89
    Cake icing, 76
    Coconut chocolate pudding, 76
cultures, 11
    purchasing starter, 98
    sourdough, 144–145
Curtido, 54–55

**D**
dairy, 92–93
    **See also** cheese
    Cultured butter, 94–95
    Cultured buttermilk, 96–97
    Greek yogurt, 104
    Kefir, 98–99
    Sour cream, 105
    Yogurt, 100–103
Date wine, 204–205
dates
    Date wine, 204–205
    Tamarind date chutney, 87
demijohns, 21
dent corn, nixtamal, 134–135
detoxification, herbs, 213
dicing, 38
digestive disorders, herbal
  remedies, 212
Dijon mustard, 79
Dosa, 120–123
dressings
    adding Dijon mustard to
      vinaigarette, 79
    Creamy horseradish salad
      dressing, 76
    Mustard vinaigerette, 76
drupes, 88–89
dulse, Seaweed sauerkraut, 50

**E**
echinacea, 213
Egyptian pickled turnips (lift),
  36–37

Egyptian preserved lemon, 34–35
English cucumbers, pickling, 30

**F**
falafel, taameyya, 37
fennel, asafoetida powder, 51
fermentation, 10–11
  bacterial, 16–17
  benefits, 14–15
  ideal environments, 24–25
  mould, 16
  origins, 12–13
  vessels, 20–21
  yeast, 17
fermented rice wine, 132
field corn, nixtamal, 134–135
fine dice, 38
fine grate, 62
Fire cider, 216
flatbread
  Dosa, 120–123
  Injera, 140–141
flavour additions, beverages, 199
flora, 15
floral flavours, beverages, 199
flu and cold, herbal remedies, 212
food dehydrators, as incubation chambers, 102
food processors, horseradish root, 73
Fresh salsa, 76

**G**
garlic, Pickled garlic, 44
ghee, 95
ginger
  grating, 41
  Pickled ginger, 45
ginger ale, 160
Ginger beer, 17, 160–161
Ginger bug, 156
  Date wine, 204–205
  Ginger beer, 160–161

Hard ginger beer, 186–187
  Mandarin wine, 200–201
glass demijohns, 21
glass kilner jars, 20
goat cheese, chevre, 110–111
gochugaru, 57
Gorditas, 138–139
grains. **See also** bread
  Amazake, 118–119
  Dosa, 120–123
  Nixtamal, 134–135
  Rejuvelac, 129
  soaking and sprouting, 126–128
  Tha bai, 132–133
  Uttapam, 124–125
grating
  ginger, 41
  techniques, 62–63
Greek yogurt, 104

**H**
habanero peppers, Wild habanero hot sauce, 82–83
Hard cider, 190–193
  Spiced hard cider, 194–195
Hard ginger beer, 186–187
herbal vinegars, 212–213
hing, 51
Hominy, 134–135
honey
  Honey mustard, 76
  Mead, 196
  Raspberry mead, 197
  raw, 179
Honey mustard, 76
horchata, amazake horchata, 164–165
horseradish root, making into paste, 73
Horseradish sauce, 73
  Creamy horseradish salad dressing, 76
  Red horseradish, 76

hot sauces
  Fresh salsa, 76
  Jalapeño hot sauce, 80–81
  Mexican, 12
  Spicy aioli, 76
  Wild habanero hot sauce, 82–83

**I**
incubation chambers, food dehydrators, 102
Indian pickling, 33
inflammation, herbal remedies, 213
Infused vinegar, 214–215
Injera, 140–141

**J**
Jalapeño hot sauce, 80–81
jalapeño peppers
  adding to sauerkraut, 46
  Jalapeño Hot Sauce, 80–81
Japanese pickled cucumber (Sunomono), 40–41
jiuqu, 132
  Sato, 202–203
Jordanian cucumbers, pickling, 30
julienne peels, creating, 63
Jun, 179

**K**
Kefir, 98–99
kefir, 17, 98–99
  Coconut milk kefir, 182–183
  Coconut water kefir, 167
  Cultured coconut cream, 88–89
  Kefir, 98–99
  Kefir champagne, 188–189
  Pineapple ginger kefir, 168–169
  Water kefir, 166
Kefir champagne, 188–189

kelp, seaweed sauerkraut, 50
ketchup
    Chipotle ketchup, 72
    Classic ketchup, 70–71
    Cocktail sauce, 76
    Mole ketchup, 72
    Quick pizza sauce, 76
Kilner jars, 20, 126
Kimchi, 13, 16, 56–59
    Pak choi white kimchi, 60–61
Kirby cucumbers, pickling, 30
kitchen colanders, 107
knife techniques, 38–39
knives, high quality, 39
koji, 119
kombu, Seaweed sauerkraut, 50
Kombucha, 17, 172–175
    Earl Grey Cherry kombucha,
    176–177
    ideal environment, 25
kvass, Beetroot kvass, 180–181

**L**
lactic acid bacteria, strained
  yogurt, 104
Lahpet (Burmese pickled tea
  leaves), 66–67
legumes
    Dosa, 120–123
    Natto, 116–117
    soaking and sprouting,
    126–127
    Tofu, 130–131
    Uttapam, 124–125
lemons
    Egyptian preserved lemon, 34–
    35
    Fire cider, 216
lentils
    Dosa, 120–123
    Uttapam, 124–125
    varieties, 120
Lift (Egyptian pickled turnips), 13,

36–37
light, fermentation, 24

**M**
Mandarin wine, 200–201
mandolins, thin slices, 63
masa, 139
Masala dosa, 122
Masala kraut, 51
Mead, 196
    Raspberry mead, 197
medium dice, 38
meze, 109
microorganisms, 11, 16-17
    beneficial bacteria, 14–15
    SCOBY (Symbiotic Colony Of
    Bacteria and Yeast), 170–171
microplanes, 62
mincing, 39
mould ferments, 16
Mole Ketchup, 72
muslin, 106–107
mustard
    Classic mustard, 74–75
    Dijon mustard, 79
    Honey mustard, 76
    Mustard vinaigrette, 76
    Sauerkraut mustard, 78
Mustard vinaigrette, 76

**N**
Natto, 16, 116–117
    ideal environment, 25
Nixtamal, 134–135
nori, Seaweed sauerkraut,
  50

**O**
odor, sauerkraut, 48
onions
    adding to sauerkraut, 46
    Continuous pickle, 32
    Sweet onion relish, 86

over-carbonation, 159
oxymel, 212–213

**P**
panela, 178
parsnips, Root kraut, 52–53
paste, creating, 39
patience, fermentation, 24
pears, Colonche, 178
peeling techniques, 63

Pickled aubergine, 65
Pickled ginger, 45
Pickled tomatoes, 64
pickling, 30–31
    Pak choi white kimchi, 60–61
    Continuous pickle, 32
    Curtido, 54–55
    Egyptian preserved lemon,
    34–35
    ideal environment, 25
    Lahpet (Burmese pickled tea
    leaves), 66–67
    Lift (Egyptian pickled turnips),
    36–37
    Masala kraut, 51
    Pickled aubergine, 65
    Pickled garlic, 44
    Pickled ginger, 45
    Pickled tomatoes, 64
    Root kraut, 52–53
    Sauerkraut, 46–49
    Seaweed sauerkraut, 50
    Sunomono (Japanese pickled
    cucumber), 40–41
    tempering, 33
    Turmeric & carrot pickles, 33
    Umeboshi (pickled ume plum),
    42–43
piloncillo, 178
pineapple
    Pineapple cider vinegar,
    208–209
    Pineapple ginger kefir, 168–169

Tepache, 162–163
Pineapple cider vinegar, 208–209
Pineapple ginger kefir, 168–169
plums, Umeboshi (pickled ume plum), 42–43
preserved lemons, 13
priming, 158
probiotics, 15
Purple amazake sourdough, 152–153

**Q–R**
Queso fresco, 112–113
Quick pizza sauce, 76

Raspberry mead, 197
Red Horseradish, 76
Red Wine Vinegar, 210–211
reduced fat milk, yogurt, 101
Rejuvelac, 129
relaxation, herbs, 213
ribbons, peeling, 63
rice
    Amazake, 118–119
    Dosa, 120–123
    Sato, 202–203
    Tha Bai, 132–133
    Uttapam, 124–125
Root kraut, 52–53
rubber bands, 107
rutabaga, root kraut, 52–53

**S**
sake, 16
salsa, Fresh salsa, 76
sanitizing fermentation vessels, 21
Sato, 17, 202–203
sauerkraut, 13, 16
    Classic sauerkraut, 46–49
    fermentation, 11
    ideal environment, 25
    Root kraut, 52–53
    Sauerkraut mustard, 78

Seaweed sauerkraut, 50
SCOBY (Symbiotic Colony Of Bacteria and Yeast), 170–171
    Earl Grey cherry kombucha, 176–177
    Jun, 179
    Kombucha, 172–175
Seaweed sauerkraut, 50
seeds, soaking and sprouting, 126–127
Shanghai yeast balls, 132
shawerma, 37
s-hooks, 106
sieves, lining with muslin, 106
slicing
    cucumbers, 30
    techniques, 63
soaking grains, legumes and seeds, 126–127
Sour cream, 105
Sourdough bread, 146–149
sourdough bread, 17
    Purple amazake sourdough, 152–153
    Sourdough bread, 146–149
    Sourdough pizza, 150–151
Sourdough pizza, 150–151
sourdough starters, 144–145
soybeans
    Natto, 16, 116–117
    Tofu, 130–131
Spiced hard cider, 194–195
Spicy aioli, 76
spicy flavours, beverages, 199
spirulina, Seaweed sauerkraut, 50
Sprouted grain, 128
sprouting grains, legumes and seeds, 126–128
starters, 11
    purchasing, 98
    sourdough, 144–145
straining yogurt, 103, 104
strawberry baskets, 107

stress, herbal remedies, 213
Sunomono (Japanese pickled cucumber), 40–41
Sweet onion relish, 86
sweetening beverages, 199
swing stopper bottles, 20

**T**
taameyya, 37
Tamarind date chutney, 87
tea
    Earl Grey cherry kombucha, 176–177
    ginger, 45
    Jun, 179
    Kombucha, 172–175
    Lahpet (Burmese pickled tea leaves), 66–67
tempeh, 16
temperature, fermentation, 24–25
tempering, 33
Tha bai, 17, 132–133
thickening yogurt, 103
Tofu, 130–131
tomatoes
    Chipotle ketchup, 72
    Classic ketchup, 70–71
    Cocktail sauce, 76
    Mole ketchup, 72
    Quick pizza sauce, 76
    Pickled tomatoes, 64
turmeric
    Turmeric & carrot pickles, 44
    white versus yellow, 33
Turmeric & carrot pickles, 33
turnips
    Lift (Egyptian pickled turnips), 36–37
    Root kraut, 52–53

**U**
ume plums, Umeboshi (pickled ume plum), 42–43
Umeboshi (pickled ume plum),

42–43
unpasteurized vinegar, 211
Uttapam, 124–125

**V**
Vegan aioli, 76
vessels
    fermentation, 20–21
    sprouting, 126
vinaigrette
    adding Dijon mustard, 79
    Mustard vinaigrette, 76
vinegar, 207
    Fire cider, 216
    ideal environment, 25
    Infused vinegar, 214–215
    making herbal, 212–213
    Pineapple cider vinegar,
      208–209
    Red wine vinegar, 210–211
    unpasteurized, 211

**W–X**
wakame, Seaweed sauerkraut, 50
water crocks, 21
Water kefir, 166
    Coconut milk kefir, 182–183
    Coconut water kefir, 167
whey
    cheese, 111
    strained yogurt, 104
white turmeric, 33
white wine vinegar, infusion, 215
whole milk, yogurt, 101
Wild habanero hot sauce, 77,
  82–83
wine, 17
    Date wine, 204–205
    fermentation, 10
    Mandarin wine, 200–201
    Red wine vinegar, 210–211
wots, 140

**Y–Z**
yeast
    ferments, 17
    SCOBY (Symbiotic Colony Of
      Bacteria and Yeast), 170–171
yellow turmeric, 33
Yogurt, 100–103
yogurt, 16
    Cultured coconut cream,
      88–89
    Greek yogurt, 104
    ideal environment, 25
    Labneh, 108–109
    straining, 104
    thickening, 103
    Yogurt, 100–103

zesting, 62
zigzag peelers, 63

## ABOUT THE AUTHOR

Adam Elabd is an educator in the fields of fermentation, natural healing, traditional food preparation, and nutrition. He's a practising herbalist whose passion for fermentation, herbs, and health is informed by his Egyptian descent and childhood spent in Saudi Arabia. He teaches classes and leads workshops on different aspects of fermentation and holistic living around California, Egypt, and parts of Europe. He is currently pursuing a Masters of Science in Nutrition at the University of Bridgeport, CT, in the US, and is conducting field research in several countries on traditional food preparation techniques.
Find Adam at www.adamelabd.com or on Instagram@adam.elabd.

## ACKNOWLEDGMENTS

Many people were involved in the creation of this book. I would like to thank my parents, who support me; my wife Yiyi, who inspires me; Maria Mendoza, who nourishes me; Darren Vandercappellen and Justin Ross Hahnson, who tested me; Arturo A. Enciso, who taught me; Diego Ortiz, who aided me; and the Anandamide Psychedelicatessen family, who match and push me in all things stinky and bubbly.

The publisher would like to thank the following for their kind permission to reproduce their photographs:

12-13 iStockphoto.com: Illustrious (map)
All other images © Dorling Kindersley
For further information see: www.dkimages.com.